Prospects

An Advanced Course
Teacher's Book

John Percil & Joanna Gray

Penguin Books

PENGUIN BOOKS

Published by the Penguin Group
27 Wrights Lane, London W8 5TZ, England
Viking Penguin Inc., 40 West 23rd Street, New York, New York 10010, USA
Penguin Books Australia Ltd, Ringwood, Victoria, Australia
Penguin Books Canada Ltd, 2801 John Street, Markham, Ontario, Canada L3R 1B4
Penguin Books (NZ) Ltd, 182–190 Wairau Road, Auckland 10, New Zealand
Penguin Books Ltd, Registered Offices: Harmondsworth, Middlesex, England

First published 1988

Printed and bound in Great Britain by
Hazell Watson & Viney Limited
Member of BPCC plc
Aylesbury, Bucks, England

CONTENTS

General Introduction   3

Unit 1   Joining   7

Unit 2   Contrasts   16

Unit 3   Logical relations   25

Unit 4   Omission   37

Unit 5   The general and the particular   47

Unit 6   Standpoint   58

Unit 7   In the negative   68

Unit 8   Emphasis   78

Unit 9   In the mind   92

Unit 10   Not quite clear   100

Alphabetical Index   102

GENERAL INTRODUCTION

This innovative advanced coursebook seeks to combine traditional teaching methods with the freer, more imaginative methods of contemporary communicative methodology. A high level of motivation is made possible by the rich variety of material and the treatment of serious subjects in depth, offering the student a genuine opportunity to develop fluency in English. Considerable responsibility is placed on the student in the belief that advanced students want to be treated as thinking adults.

Concentrated practice within a broadly designated area of structure and lexis, and constant unannounced re-cycling, are features of the course.

ORGANISATION

Each of the ten units consists of the following six sections:

A Reading Texts	B Communicative Activities	C Listening Activities	D Structure and Language Usage	E Writing Activities	Study Notes
home	classroom (preceded by Study Notes [home])	class	class (preceded by Study Notes [home])	home	home

A   READING

The reading texts should be prepared by the students, working at home, before the work on the unit is started. They must, therefore, be set as the previous unit is completed.

The texts are from a variety of British and American modern and historical sources. They include famous short stories, scientific and sociological articles, a literary essay, extracts from popular magazines, from an essay on art history, and from two books on politics. The more complex or abstract texts occur in the later units.

Teachers who wish to exploit the texts beyond the ways suggested will find that they readily lend themselves to further exploitation without deviating from the broad theme of the unit. (For example, Text A of Unit 7 could lead on to discussions about what individuals or families keep secret and why, or in vocabulary/structure terms to other items on the pattern of the negative vocabulary of various types to be found in the text: e.g. 'of no benefit', 'non-release', 'far from clear', 'no such procedure'.)

Procedure

Divide your group into Groups A and B: Group A read Text A for homework and Group B read Text B. They should *not* read each other's texts at this stage. (In the case of the relatively short texts of Unit 1, these may be read silently in class if there is no time to set homework before starting the book.) Otherwise for all units follow the instructions as · set out on page 5. Make sure that (b) and (c) are done as fully as possible; help students to formulate or answer questions as necessary.

B COMMUNICATIVE ACTIVITIES

(Always alert students to the topics that are going to be considered and set the relevant Study Notes as homework before tackling this section. Should this be impossible in the case of the first unit, allow students to work on the Study Notes for 5–10 minutes in class.)

Note the use of symbols in the Student's Book to give an immediate indication of how the students are to group themselves, or what kind of activity they are going to carry out.

Students work in pairs

It is suggested that this should mean that students tackle the activity initially in pairs (or, in a very small group, individually) and then, when they have formulated their responses, compare them with those of the other pairs and so complete the activity as *one* group.

Students work as a group

Activities to be handled in this way are generally those which are not considered to need quite so much preparatory work; however, if the level or relatively high numbers of the group demand it, these activities should be done initially as pairwork, with students moving to completion of the activity working as one group.

C LISTENING ACTIVITIES

Listening is treated as an integral element in the communication process rather than as an adjunct. For this reason, activities are varied in theme and are designed to promote the natural discussion which usually follows a shared listening experience.

Each unit gives the teacher information on the particular theme, objective, activity and role of the teacher.

Tapescripts are not printed in the Student's Book, so it is essential that the teacher should listen to the cassette and study the tapescript before introducing the listening material. If no cassette recorder is available, the teacher can read from the tapescript, perhaps with a colleague (for dialogues).

D STRUCTURE AND LANGUAGE USAGE

This section provides intensive controlled practice in the vocabulary, structures and sometimes functions which are closely linked to the theme of the unit. It is of particular importance that students prepare the relevant Study Notes carefully before tackling this work in class. Of course this section does not all have to be done at the point it occurs in the book, but could profitably be used to provide a change of pace and activity at an earlier point in the unit, for example between Communicative Activities in B, and then re-cycled until a high degree of accuracy is achieved.

E   WRITING ACTIVITIES

These offer consolidation and/or extension of the unit activities and would normally be set as homework before the end of the unit was reached. Teachers should be aware of the fact that this section often involves a considerable amount of work and that consequently some students may need to start thinking about it at a relatively early point in the unit.

STUDY NOTES

These give students useful vocabulary, particularly for the Communicative Activities (B) and transfer work as preparation mainly for the Structure and Usage section (D). They are a key component of the book, and students should be urged to take them very seriously. Whilst it is not intended to prescribe the use of particular vocabulary, students will find it of great benefit to focus on the relevant area of language before taking part in the classroom activities. This process of familiarisation should normally be done at home and would involve checking on the meaning, pronunciation and usage of the vocabulary involved with the assistance of a good English–English dictionary.

Note that it is not necessary to work through the book from Unit 1 to Unit 10; teachers may, with some classes, wish to work through the material in a different order. However the longer texts do appear in the later units. Note also that more than one answer is possible to many of the questions: suggested answers only are provided. And teacher support is not always needed or given to the Writing Activities.

Cambridge 1988   John Percil
London 1988   Joanna Gray

1 JOINING

Themes	Marriage, love, friendship, groups and organisations, compromises
Functions	Enumerating, talking about relationships, proposing compromises
Structures	Infinitive of purpose, non-defining relatives, apposition, participles. Should, must, have to. 'Open: compounds; structures with' even if; unless; even; even though; however; despite; or . . . otherwise. Verb patterns: agree, disagree
Phonology	1 Weak forms of should, must, have to. Contrasts.
	Examples: I should have known. (weak)
	Why *should* you? (strong)
	I must be going. (weak)
	You *must* have known. (strong)
	2 Rhythm and intonation of non-defining relative clauses.
	Examples: Our company, which was founded in 1896, has carried on its tradition of service. Members of the company, many of whom have agreed to reductions in wages, are the chief asset.
	Note that this usage is more often found in the written or formal spoken form. Commas can be used as pause indicators, with falling intonation.
Lexis	unification, alloy (n), compound (n), coalition, merge, merger, fusion, synthesis, blend, bring together, synthesise, amalgamate, link (v), alliance, union, federation

A READING TEXTS

1 READING

Enumerating skills (Text B, page 169)

Before (C) is attempted, alert students to the need for a varied 'introduction' to each paragraph.
Examples: Then at the age of . . . Then we came to early adolescence, when friendship . . . *It's the early 20s that are the peak . . . When we get to the late 20s and early 30s*, however . . . *On the other hand . . .* the 40s . . . *Much later, in the post-retirement period . . .* (Examples could be put on the board.)

B COMMUNICATIVE ACTIVITIES

1 MARRIAGE

Students work as a group. Encourage a free and lively discussion. (This activity may not be of interest to all groups. If it's not, it should be omitted.)

Suggested supplementary questions

What is the difference between admiration and love? Why is it important to share the same background? Would you include agreement about friends in your list of pointers? Isn't it dangerous for a relationship if one partner dislikes the other's friends?

2 FRIENDS

Students work as a group.

Suggested supplementary questions

ii   For example, if your wife/husband kept a diary, would you feel you had the right to read it? Do you read each other's letters?
iv   If this is considered impossible: Isn't it a bit cynical to think that any friendship with a member of the opposite sex must have a sexual element?
         If this is considered possible: Don't we deceive ourselves when we think we can? Isn't a sexual element always there?

3 GROUPS

Students work as a group. Encourage students to offer more than one possibility wherever they can.

a
   i   BMA (British Medical Association), AAUP (American Association of University Professors)
   ii   CND (Campaign for Nuclear Disarmament), RSPCA (Royal Society for the Prevention of Cruelty to Animals)
   iii   golf clubs; dramatic societies

b   *Possible answers (names of groups)*
    i   trade unions
    ii   Boy Scouts, Sea Cadets, Cadet Force (military training at school), adventure
            courses (e.g. climbing, canoeing etc. in Scotland); some boarding schools that
            emphasize sport, leadership skills etc.
    iii   Red Cross (or Red Crescent)
    iv   the Mafia
    v   secret services, information services, e.g. CIA, KGB, MI5 (UK)
    vi   consumer associations
    vii   the Campaign for Nuclear Disarmament

Extension

One student describes what an organisation does and the rest of the group have to
identify it. Elicit local examples.

4   MAKING COMPROMISES

Students work as a group.

Possible answers (examples only)

a   Let's say £425, shall we, and 10% discount?
b   I know I can listen to the radio on the earphone; I'll sleep in the other bed just for
     tonight; I'll use the little torch.
c   Can we say ten now and a further ten in six months' time?
d   OK, you can choose *some* of your clothes.
e   I propose the flights should be at two-week intervals in the other Superpower's
     planes.
f   You read my letters and I'll read your diary; If you don't read my letters, I will not
     read your diary.

5   APHORISMS AND SAYINGS ABOUT LOVE

Students work as a group. Encourage students to give examples wherever possible,
particularly when the meaning is clear, as in v and vi.

Possible answers (examples only)

b
    i   Relationships are always unequal: one partner is active, the other passive.
            One loves and the other loves being loved; one partner always loves the other
            partner more than he or she is loved.
    ii   True love doesn't try to control or manipulate; rather it allows the other to grow
            and develop in new directions.
    iii   Very few people have any experience of so-called true love; True love only
            exists in the minds of a few (deluded?) individuals.
    iv   If you love or don't love somebody, it very soon becomes obvious.
    v   Women make men want to achieve more, but by their demands on them for
            time, money etc. stop them making any real progress.

vi   When you first love someone you feel nervous or excited when you are alone together, and when love dies you have nothing to say to each other.

vii   Friendship and love are two totally different feelings, the former never growing into the latter.

viii Love is two people linked in their hope; and looking outwards towards life not/interested only in each other/obsessed with each other.

6   THE —— THAT'S GOT EVERYTHING!

Students work in pairs. Ensure that students produce completions of the right kind, always beginning with a noun or pronoun (e.g. the *city* that, the *one* that . . .)

Possible answers (examples only)

a

i   the sophisticated city; the city that charms.
ii   the number one card; the one the whole world knows.
iii   a country of unrivalled beauty and hospitality.
iv   the cat-food voted No. 1 by the nation's top cats.
v   Switzerland's best-kept secret; the ski resort with style.
vi   the connoisseur's airline; the airline that cares.
vii   the world's choice; the car with the big name.
viii the businessman's private palace; the hotel with everything; the big hotel that treats you like an individual/a person.
ix   the only way; the way a woman likes it said.
x   the no-nonsense newspaper; the paper with a mind as well as a heart.

7   TWO-PART ADVERTISEMENTS AND SLOGANS

Students work as a group.

Possible answers (examples only)

a   Choose Intasun and don't pay more than necessary; Intasun have got the most competitive prices.

b   Buy Hoover and buy the best; The best domestic appliances are produced by Hoover; Hoover are No. 1.

c   It tastes great and it's only one calorie; It's got a good taste but without too many calories.

d   Sealink has connections with more destinations (than its competitors); Travel by Sealink to lots more destinations.

e   A nuclear state inevitably becomes a police state; If a country goes nuclear it can't avoid being/becoming a police state.

C LISTENING ACTIVITIES

The *theme* is interaction in problem-solving. The *objective* is to begin group formation through shared activity.

The activity has three parts:

Part 1   Students are asked to form groups of three to ten members, the size of the group depending on the judgement of the teacher. They then study the photographs and discuss how the bottles could have been filled.

Part 2   Students listen to the first recorded problem. Then they work in their original groups to answer the questions (in their books) and any other questions which may come up. Group activity is then shared with the entire class.

Part 3   The same procedure as for Part 2.

The teacher has to set the ground rules for Part 1, and these rules should be followed throughout the groups' activities:

1   Only one person can speak at any one time.
2   Members are not allowed to criticise or evaluate the opinions of others.
3   The groups should appoint notetakers and leaders.
4   The notetaker will list ideas and report back to the group should there be confusion.
5   The leader should begin and end the activity and be prepared to report back to the class. It is important to set time limits.

The role of the teacher is to monitor group activities without influencing opinions and to draw the groups together at the end of the activity.

Tapescript

2   Henry Adams worked in a tall office block. Every morning he got into the lift on the ground floor, pressed the lift button to the eleventh floor, got out and walked up to the sixteenth floor. Every night he got into the lift on the sixteenth floor and took the lift all the way to the ground floor.

3   A suspected break-in occurred at number 41 Rose Walk last night. On the ground floor, a quantity of broken glass was discovered, the carpet was wet and a window was slightly open. The deceased were identified as Antony and Cleopatra. Police are asking members of the public to cooperate in helping to solve this incident.

D STRUCTURE AND LANGUAGE USAGE

1 STUDENTS WORK AS A GROUP

Do this as a round-the-class exercise.

Possible answers

a

   i   Henry Moore, a world-famous sculptor, died in 1986 at the age of 88; Henry Moore, who was a world- famous sculptor . . .

   ii   Henry Moore, who was influenced by primitive African and Mexican art, died in . . .

   iii   Henry Moore, before whom there were no British sculptors of comparable stature, died in 1986 at the age . . .

b

   i   Aberdeen, situated between the mouths of the Rivers Don and Dee, has in recent years become . . .; Aberdeen, which is situated between the mouths of . . .

   ii   Aberdeen, which has a population of 200,000, has in recent years . . .; Aberdeen, with a population of 200,000, has in recent years . . .

   iii   Aberdeen, where some important research institutes have been established, has in recent years become an important . . .

c

   i   The Bank of England, nicknamed 'The Old Lady of Threadneedle Street', was founded in 1694; The Bank of England, whose nickname is 'The Old Lady of Threadneedle Street', was founded in 1694.

   ii   The Bank of England, which was a private institution before 1946, was founded in 1694.

   iii   The Bank of England, the main function of which is to act as a central bank, was founded in 1694; The Bank of England, whose main function is to act as a central bank . . .

d

   i   Ten new oil-fired power-stations are being built, three of which are almost finished.

   ii   Ten new oil-fired power-stations are being built, which will bring the total up to 53; Ten new oil-fired power-stations are being built, bringing the total up to 53.

   iii   Ten new oil-fired power-stations are being built, most of which are located in the north of the country; Ten new oil-fired power-stations are being built, most of them (being) in the north of the country.

e

   i   Bertrand Russell, (the) author of *Principia Mathematica*, was one of the greatest philosophers of his time; Bertrand Russell, who was the author of *Principia Mathematica*, was one of the greatest . . .

   ii   Bertrand Russell, who was imprisoned for his pacifism in 1918, was one of the greatest . . .

   iii   Bertrand Russell, who was awarded the Nobel Prize for literature in 1950, was one of the greatest philosophers of his time.

f

    i   Consumer spending, which is boosted by strong growth in real incomes, is expected to remain at record levels in the coming months; Consumer spending, boosted by strong growth in real incomes, is expected to remain . . .; Boosted by strong growth in real incomes, consumer spending is expected to remain . . .

    ii   Consumer spending, particularly on consumer durables, is expected . . .

    iii   Consumer spending, particularly that on consumer durables . . .

g

    i   Nobody seemed to notice Celia's engagement ring or her new dress, which annoyed her; It annoyed her that nobody seemed . . .

    ii   Nobody seemed to notice Celia's engagement ring or her new dress, instead of which they talked about her brother's car and his recent promotion.

h

    i   Concorde, which was built by the French and British, came into service in 1976; Concorde, built by . . .

    ii   Concorde, the cost of which was borne by French and British taxpayers, came into service in 1976; Concorde, whose cost was borne . . .

    iii   Concorde, only twenty of which were built, came into service in 1976.

2

Students work as a group. Where there is more than one possibility, alert students to the fact (e.g. a, c, g) or give possible vocabulary as cues.

Possible answers

a   Every year they attend a special blessing in church to give thanks for their union.

b   It's difficult to describe their music accurately – I suppose it's a synthesis/blend/fusion of blues and Brazilian music.

c   She made it to the top because she had a blend of courage and amazing determination.

d   After a weekend of intense political speculation, the three main parties agreed to form a coalition.

e   The word 'playboy' is a compound of (the words) 'play' and 'boy'.

f   The island is linked to the mainland by twice-weekly air services and a monthly ferry; Twice-weekly air services and a monthly ferry link the/island to the mainland/mainland to the island/island and mainland; The island and the mainland are linked by . . .

g   There's a club in most larger cities, so now they've decided to form a federation with offices in London.

h   In many ways it's entirely logical that there should be a merger between them. In product range . . .; In many ways it's entirely logical that the two should have merged. In product range . . .

i   Cavour worked for the unification of Italy; Cavour worked to achieve the unification of Italy.

j   The broad aim of the conference was to bring together experts working in the same technical area so that they could exchange expertise.

k   In his present work he's trying to bring together several prominent themes of his previous work into a new synthesis; In his present work he's trying to synthesize/blend several prominent themes of his previous work (into a new whole).

l   In view of the growing threat from larger neighbours, these three countries quickly/decided on an/formed an/came together in an/alliance.

m   Their wine has been carefully blended with wine from other areas to produce a smoother taste.

n   Aluminium bronze is an alloy of aluminium and copper.

3   MAKING COMPOUNDS

Take every opportunity to alert students to note examples of these 'open compounds' in what they read and try to use, or what they write whenever possible. Of course, the compounds are particularly useful in such passages as a summary, where brevity is extremely important.

a   Students work in pairs.

b   Students work as a group.

Possible answers

i   *Road-haulage fuel costs* are still rising.
ii   *Fashion trade textile manufacturers* are experiencing difficult market conditions.
iii *The July unemployment figures* show a slight rise on June.
iv   *Daytime electricity consumption* has risen by 65% since 1986.
v   *Government inflation forecasts* have been consistently wrong in recent years.
vi   *August High Street spending* tops £7 billion.
vii The *1985–6 ICI reorganisation* is now beginning to bear fruit.
viii *Open University computer technology courses* have doubled in number in only two years.

E WRITING ACTIVITIES

1

Possible answer

Married for ten years, during which Paul's income had expanded, Jessica had only recently gone back to work after having two children. Their relationship had always been a stormy one but it was certainly never boring. However, as Paul's authority and power grew at work, so did his desire to get his own way at home, making their relationship even stormier at a time when Jessica was trying to cope with a new job as well as taking care of the children. Jessica's feelings and opinions were treated with scant respect, and she responded by having a series of short-term affairs with men she met through work.

The crisis came when Paul insisted on moving to a very grand, expensive home in an exclusive district. Jessica didn't want to move, but her opinion was ignored. Without the sense of support she gained from her former neighbours and local friends, she decided that there wasn't much point left in the marriage and the couple eventually split up.

Jessica and Paul's marriage failed because Paul refused to take his wife's feelings and anxieties seriously. He was incapable of resolving tricky issues except by insisting on his own way and although Jessica constantly asked him, he refused to talk through marriage problems with a counsellor. Unfortunately, Jessica wasn't very persistent, preferring to take the easy way out of necessary confrontations by turning to a series of short-term lovers instead. If the couple had talked to a counsellor, their strong feelings for each other could have been channelled into making their marriage work.

2   PREFIXES

b

i   out
       Examples: outlive, outplay, outmanoeuvre, outdo.
ii   counter
       Examples: counterbalance, counterdemand, countercheck.
iii   mal
       Examples: malfunction, malform, malpractice.
iv   mis
       Examples: misunderstand, mistrust, misrepresentation.
v   hyper
       Examples: hypercritical, hyperactive, hypersensitive.
vi   co
       Examples: cooperate, co-ownership, coincidence.
vii   over
       Examples: overdo, over-complicated, overwork.
viii   pre
       Examples: predate, pre-school, prerequisite.
ix   inter
       Examples: interrelate, inter-company, interdependence.

Preparation of Reading Texts A and B for the next unit should now be set, as homework, and done before work on the next unit is begun. This should be done for every unit.

2 CONTRASTS

Themes	Social divisions, intelligence, examinations 1936–86
Functions	Making comparisons, drawing distinctions, 'disarming'
Structures	Comparatives, concessive 'may' and 'might'. Structures with 'although,' 'even though,' 'despite,' 'in spite of,' 'nevertheless,' 'whereas,' 'unlike,' 'even if,' 'rather than,' yet ☐
Phonology	Weak forms of from/to. Rhythm and syllable stress as in: contrary to ☐ ☐ ☐ . . ./in contrast to. . . ./ as opposed to . ./ distinct from . . .
Lexis	distinct from, contrary to, in contrast to, by contrast, as opposed to, without distinction, to differentiate, distinguish, make distinctions, discriminate, differ
	ideally, theoretically, superficially, outwardly, officially, technically

A READING TEXTS

1 READING

'The lesson we refuse to learn' was written at a time when government policies under Mrs Thatcher seemed to many people actually to be encouraging a greater degree of social divisiveness than had occurred in Britain for more than thirty years.

Christian names like Emma, Daphne, or Amanda suggest membership of the middle classes, whereas Tracy or Darren would probably be working-class.

Text A

Encourage students to employ their enumerating skills practised in Unit 1 in stating what the various contrasts are between the two social groups referred to.

B COMMUNICATIVE ACTIVITIES

1 CLASS CONSCIOUSNESS

Students work as a group.

a

Suggested supplementary questions

Why do you think it has changed (if it has)? How has this change come about?

c

Encourage students to use their dictionaries, and give them ample time to consider their answers. Give key words, such as 'display', 'achieve', 'regard', where necessary.

Possible answers

i	Ways of displaying your class; items like expensive cars that show the class you belong to or aspire to belong to.
ii	A social system in which people achieve position on merit and merit only.
iii	People who regard themselves as socially superior to others/who look down on most other people.
iv	Moving up socially/the social ladder/into the next social class/into the class above.
v	People who haven't been rich very long/who have made their money in industry/business.
vi	A feeling of antagonism between classes; lack of understanding between different sections of the community.
vii	To show respect for your 'social betters'; to defer to your 'social superiors'.
viii	To begrudge other people their (superior) opportunities and position; to resent the fact that other people have a superior lifestyle.

d

Suggested supplementary questions

What about changes in a circle of friends? Does the lifestyle of their children change?

f

Suggested supplementary questions

Will there always be class systems? Do we in fact need them? Wouldn't life be rather colourless without them?

2   CONTRASTS IN INTELLIGENCE

a   Students work as a group. If some time has elapsed since reading Text B, students should be allowed to re-read the text briefly before they answer.

b   Students work as a group. John Holt, for example, seems to have a very active and healthy view of intelligence. He seems to distrust the lonely introvert type of person.

Suggested supplementary question

If you were very imaginative and living in a fantasy world (you might be an artist of some kind), wouldn't you be intelligent, in John Holt's opinion?

c   Students work in pairs. According to numbers, distribute items among pairs of students who then think about their 'definitions'. When they give their definition of, e.g. 'a good brain', elicit contrasts by asking them, e.g. 'So what's the difference between that and a "trained mind"?' 'How does that differ from "understanding"?'

d   Students work as a group.

e   Students work as a group.

Possible answers

   i   an analytical mind; inventive skills; practical intelligence; problem-solving skills; visualizing ability
   ii   genius; great understanding; creative power; imagination; intelligence
   iii   very shrewd; practical intelligence; business acumen; judgement; insight; 'able to think on his feet'
   iv   creative intelligence; visualizing ability
   v   insight; judgement; imagination; shrewdness
   vi   analytical mind; practical intelligence
   vii   spiritual perception; insight; great understanding

f   Students work as a group.

g   Students work as a group.

3   PAST AND PRESENT

a   *Contrasts between examinations 1936–86*

Students work in pairs. Give students plenty of time to look at the two examinations and form pairs to work out their answers to (i)–(iv).

Possible answers

i   One tests literary skills, whereas the other tests the ability to make logical deductions/reason logically.

ii, iii(a)   There has been a cultural change/shift away from literacy towards numeracy. At that time a good English style and a knowledge of English literature were considered the signs of/an educated/a cultured mind. Nowadays/we have a more functional view of language/there is less emphasis on good written style.

iii(b) A lot of the more routine tasks have been taken over by developments in information technology. There is much more emphasis now on 'the skills for the job'. Therefore an administrator needs logical reasoning more than 'a cultured mind'. A lot of offices have been computerized.

iv   Give students some time to look at questions 1 and 2 in 1986 Test.

Answers

1   (e)   2

Suggested supplementary question

Can you express in words what the pattern is?

4   CONTRASTS EXPRESSED IN PROVERBS AND QUOTATIONS

a   Students work in pairs. According to numbers, distribute the proverbs etc. among pairs and give them a little time to prepare their answers.

Possible answers

i   We always feel that if we changed our circumstances everything might improve for us; Other people are having a better time than we are.

ii   The important thing is to learn from experience, not just to have it.

iii   Men and women admire very different qualities in men.

iv   Everyone feels the need for a different (more complete?) kind of love.

v   Fear prevents us from fulfilling our (optimistic) promises.

vi   The military mind is not usually very intelligent.

vii Relationships start with romance for women but decline into domestic service.

b   Students work as a group.

C LISTENING ACTIVITIES

1

The *theme* is contrasts in perception and approach. The *objective* is to promote a problem-solving activity in which a common language (English) must be used.

The activity has three parts:

Part 1   Stop the tape after section a and b and give students an opportunity to discuss possible answers. The lecturer's solution to section a is provided on tape. Encourage a range of questions, such as: 120 what? . . . years? kilos? hours? pounds? They will say that they need more information.

Part 2   Listening for context and meaning is emphasised.

The teacher becomes a facilitator.

In Part 1 any answer is acceptable so long as it is relevant. Students should not be allowed to devalue other students' contributions.

In Part 2, there are certain key words which students should notice in the example and carry on with.

2

Suggested answers

Example:	Lateral	Vertical
	Creative Jump ahead	Selective Sequential
	Hypothetical allowed	Each step correct before proceeding
	Unconventional, enquiring approach	Obvious, conventional approach
	Changing labels	Fixed labels
	Process	Solution

Remember that both approaches are useful and complementary.

3

Students work as a group.

Tapescript

Male voice

a   You have invited me here today to introduce the concept of lateral thinking. Let me say first that I do not intend this to be a conventional lecture. I shall be asking you to participate.

Having established the 'ground rules', as it were, let us proceed to the subject. Since most of us have been trained to think vertically . . . and believe this way of thinking to be the only effective form, it is my initial task to address the contrasts between vertical and lateral thinking. First, vertical thinking selects what appears to be the best way of looking at a problem. Lateral thinking creates many alternative approaches. There is an old riddle which could illustrate these different approaches to problem-solving. When you have heard it, try to find a solution.

A man worked in a tall office building. Each morning he got into the lift on the ground floor, pressed the lift button to the eleventh floor, got out of the lift and walked up to the sixteenth floor. At night he would get into the lift on the sixteenth floor and get out on the ground floor. What was the reason for this?

b   No doubt you are waiting for *my* answer. Well, here it is. The man was a dwarf and couldn't reach higher than the eleventh-floor button. The natural assumption is that the *man* is normal and the behaviour is *ab*normal. In fact, it is just the opposite.

Let us continue with other contrasts. When we think vertically, we move in sequential steps . . . rather like an old man climbing a ladder. In lateral thinking, it is possible to jump ahead and then fill in the gaps later. The solution may make sense, even though the pathway is not vertical. It is certainly true that scientific research is often based on vertical thinking. However, the discovery of penicillin and its life-saving developments were the result of lateral thinking.

Another difference is that vertical thinking implies that each problem-solving step must be correct before the next can be approached. Think back to the way you learned mathematics. Addition, subtraction, multiplication, division. Were you asked to show the process, even when the result was correct? Indeed, mathematics could not function without this discipline. Lateral thinking differs in that it is possible to generate a range of hypothetical solutions without providing steps of the process. Shall we try an example? Right. Here is the answer. One hundred and twenty. Now try to find questions that might generate this answer.

c   I trust that your activity has illustrated my point: there are many different ways of reaching the same destination. However, we must now conclude with further aspects of lateral and vertical thinking. Let me pose a question. Is the tomato a fruit or a vegetable? In vertical thinking, we use fixed categories, whereas in lateral thinking labels may change according to our experience and point of view. Botanically, the tomato is a fruit. Do you expect to find tomatoes in a fruit salad? Most probably not. But the ubiquitous tomato will appear in every *vegetable* salad.

A tendency in vertical thinking is to examine the obvious approach and exclude what seems to be irrelevant. I well remember, when planning a business trip from Bilbao to Vigo, the advice I received from a Spanish colleague: 'It's not the distance but the time.' He was a lateral thinker. Vertical thinking, by its nature, is in search of one final answer. Lateral thinkers are aware that there may be no answer at all.

Finally, and you must be wondering whether you will be able to *think* tomorrow, the differences are fundamental and the thought processes are distinct. But never forget that neither process can be discarded. Both are useful. . Both are necessary. They are complementary.

D STRUCTURE AND LANGUAGE USAGE

1 THE LANGUAGE OF CONTRAST

Students work as a group. Treat this as a round-the-class exercise. It is particularly important that students should have looked at the Study Notes *before* attempting it.

Possible answers

a

  i   Everybody's advised against doing it, but (nevertheless) I'm (nevertheless) still going ahead (nevertheless).

  ii   Even though everybody's advised against doing it, I'm still going ahead.

b

  i   Whereas fifty years ago people used to make their own entertainment, nowadays they sit . . .

  ii   Unlike fifty years ago, when people used to make their own entertainment, nowadays they sit passively in front of their television.

c

  i   Despite their promise to have it . . .

  ii   In spite of their promise to have it . . .

d

  i   Even though it isn't ideal, it's the best in the circumstances.

  ii   It might not be ideal, but it's the best . . .

e

  i   Even if he is very gifted, he needn't be so rude.

  ii   He may be very gifted, but he needn't be so rude.

f

  i   He likes jazz and country and western, unlike his wife who prefers soul and reggae./Unlike his wife, who prefers soul and reggae, he likes jazz and country and western.

  ii   He likes jazz and country and western; his wife on the other hand prefers soul and reggae./Whereas he likes jazz and country and western, his wife, on the other hand prefers soul and reggae.

g

  i   The new manager's approach differs from his predecessor's/that of his predecessor.

  ii   The new manager's approach contrasts with his predecessor's/that of his predecessor.

h

  i   I can't differentiate between soul and reggae.

  ii   I can't distinguish between soul and reggae; I can't distinguish soul from reggae.

i

    i   There should be no distinction(s) in the way members of the club are treated.

    ii   There should be no difference(s) in the way members of the club are treated.

j

    i   I'm not sure you've always discriminated between 'explanation' and 'process'.

    ii   I'm not sure you've always made/kept/maintained a distinction between 'explanation' and 'process'.

2   BUT . . .

a   Students work as a group. Encourage students to offer as many possibilities as they can.

Possible answers (examples only)

    i   . . . but it would take a lot of time and money; but there would be problems.

    ii   . . . but you soon realise that he really is rather odd / strange; but you soon realize it's only a mask.

    iii   . . . but inside he was shaking like a leaf; but inwardly he was in turmoil.

    iv   . . . but in fact he's in Brighton; but he's really at home.

    v   . . . but his temperament is suspect/lets him down.

b   In everyday conversation you frequently hear expressions such as 'I don't want to bother you, but . . .', 'I hope I'm not interrupting, but . . .', 'Don't think me nosey, will you, but . . .', 'I don't wish to be interfering, but wouldn't it be a good idea if you . . .' The term *disarmers* has been suggested for them because their purpose seems to be to anticipate possible objections. Thus, 'I don't want to bother you, but . . .' may be an attempt to stop the other person saying, 'Can't you see I'm busy?' or something similar. All the examples in (b) can be regarded in this way. Possible Answers g to j (above) are typical of public speech or lecture style. The kind of contrast varies: eg. in (1) it lies in the fact that you do exactly what you say you don't want to do, i.e. you say you don't want to bother somebody and then immediately disturb them. It would be a useful exercise to collect further examples or make them up by thinking of objections such as 'It's too expensive' or 'It's irrelevant', and turning them into 'disarmers': 'Some of you may think that this is too expensive, but I think it's worth every penny!' or 'To some this might seem irrelevant, but I claim it is absolutely crucial.'

    Students work in pairs. Encourage students to offer several alternatives for each and exploit any possibilities for humour.

Possible answers (examples only)

    i   . . . (but) are you thinking of getting married?

    ii   . . . (but) are you sure you love him as much as he loves you?

    iii   . . . (but) I'd prefer not to be reminded every few days.

    iv   . . . when did you buy that dress?

    v   . . . (but) are you sure you're not making a big mistake?

    vi   . . . (but) could I have some more of that delicious pie?

    vii .,. . (but) is this really the best way of going about it?

    viii . . . (but) who was that man I saw you with?

E WRITING ACTIVITIES

2 EXTENSION: TEXT IMPROVEMENT

Possible answer

At all the other Grand Prix this season the weather had been perfect. Here in Adelaide there was the constant threat of rain. Mansell had his problems at the starts of the other races whereas everything went perfectly for him in preparation for his championship bid.

In Mexico his Honda engine had been tuned to deliver 1,100 horsepower but over here, even though it was set to produce appreciably less, Mansell was still faster, recording by far the best average speed in practice and achieving the starting position he wanted. Mansell's two rivals for the World Championship both had to win to have a chance while Mansell only had to come third to clinch it. It seemed that with only 10 minutes to go and in third place, Mansell was sitting pretty but fate then dealt the favourite a cruel blow when his tyre blew up at 200 mph. Instead of slamming on the brakes and holding the wheel rigid as you or I would have done, he zigzagged to a controlled stop, lucky to be alive.

Preparation of Texts A and B should be set as homework before the next unit is attempted.

3 LOGICAL RELATIONS

Themes	The roots of football hooliganism, body language, the visual representation of information, past and present, scenarios
Functions	Adducing causes, challenging assumptions, expressing tentativeness. Expressing deductions
Structure	Conditionals, modals (should, ought, must, need, could, might, will). Participles; Seeing that . . . Standards having fallen in recent years. . . . resulting from . . . Verb patterns (necessitate, mean, involve, aim, prevent, intend) In case, since (reason), unless. Used to (do). It's better to . . . make somebody (do)
Phonology	Noun / verb syllable stress shift; e.g. object (n), object (v); address (n), address (v). Compounds. Difference in word stress and meaning between adjectival and noun usage. For example, smoking compartment ; smoking-compartment; singing teacher (a teacher who is singing); singing-teacher (a teacher of singing)
Lexis	A result of . . .; lead to . . .; prevent; means (n), mean (v), bring about, cause (v and n), effect (n), affect (v), achieve, target (n), goal, purpose, objective, conclusion, aim (v), motive, motivation, incentive, necessary, necessitate, shape (v), lie behind, deliberately, intentional, involve, conducive to, associated with, consequences, conclusion

A READING TEXTS

1 READING

Text B is shorter than Text A but contains some difficult scientific vocabulary that will need special attention. When Group B are telling Group A about their text, it may be convenient to ask three pairs of students to recount one theory each. Encourage students to sequence the material.

Example: Firstly . . . / One theory is that . . .

                 The second theory . . . / Then there's the theory that . . .

                 The third theory . . . / On the other hand, Harold Urey . . .

2 QUESTIONS ON THE TEXTS

Students may need help with this.

Text B

Students work in pairs. Give pairs plenty of time to prepare their answers, either in class or as homework. Answers should include the following facts, and students may decide others are also important (this is a very tightly condensed version):

Simple organic molecules (e.g. proteins, amino acids) were formed from the atmosphere as a result of solar radiation. The first cells with the ability to communicate information to succeeding generations are thought to have originated in the sea and then, about 40 million years ago, to have moved to the land, where a build-up of oxygen made life possible.

B COMMUNICATIVE ACTIVITIES

1 INFLUENCES

Students work as a group.

a
Suggested questions

How was that influence communicated? Was it a very direct influence or indirect? Did your parents influence you by example or by 'instruction'?

b Encourage the use of 'should', 'ought', 'it's better to'.
Suggested supplementary question

Are you grateful for those influences or are there some that you resent?

c
Suggested supplementary question

Do you consider it likely that your ideas will be fundamentally changed by experience?

d
Suggested supplementary question (depending on student responses)

Do you think that you should influence them in a very different way so that they can cope with a changed environment? How would you do so?

2 CAUSAL LINKS

a

Students work as a group. Encourage the use of a variety of structures, including conditionals. Teachers may wish to pre-teach some of the italicised items below.

Possible answers (examples only)

i   Social deprivation leads to/*causes*/*creates* high crime rates.
ii   A happy childhood *leads to*/*is likely to lead to*/*is conducive to* a happy adulthood; If you have a happy childhood you are likely to have a happy adulthood.
iii Junk food *causes*/*is said to lead to* disturbed behaviour in children. Junk food *has been established as a cause of* disturbed behaviour in children.
iv   Sightings of UFOs *have been taken as*/*considered evidence for* life in another part of the universe.
v   Violence on TV, video and films *is often held responsible for* the increasing number of crimes of violence. If people see violence on TV, video, and in films they are more likely to commit crimes of violence themselves.
vi   Some *see* the increasing wealth of the West *as causing* poverty and starvation in developing countries.

Suggested supplementary questions

How exactly does social deprivation affect crime rates? What category of crime in particular? Why is it that a happy childhood is conducive to a happy adulthood? Is it really? How does junk food affect behaviour? Where do you think UFOs come from?/Do you think people imagine they see them?/pretend to have seen them? But doesn't it *help* people to get rid of their violent feelings just by watching violence? Why are the rich getting richer and the poor getting poorer?

Further possibility

Repeat the activity, starting with the *second* item e.g. High crime rates are the result of social deprivation. (Omit (iv).)

b   *Interrelations*

Students work as a group. Check that vocabulary e.g. *real incomes, research* is known. As in (a) above, encourage variety of structure and also encourage *tentativeness* where the causal link is less clear-cut e.g. . . . real income *might well*/*would probably*/*could* come down./'*might be associated with* a fall in . . .' instead of 'comes down'. *Education* in (3) may be interpreted in several ways such as *the need for educational places* or *average educational* levels.

Possible answers (examples only)

i As retail prices go up inflation and money incomes will probably increase but real incomes might remain the same or actually fall. When money incomes increase inflation and retail prices might rise with them; but real incomes could remain steady or fall. A rise in real incomes might be associated with a fall in both retail prices and inflation but possibly a rise in money incomes.

ii A drop in investment in research and development will probably have the effect of slowing down technological advances in industry, which will eventually affect company profits. Increases in company profits make investment in research and development more possible, which will encourage technological advances in industry.

iii If the birth rate goes up there will be more need for educational provision/there is a need for more educational places. Rises in average educational levels are often associated with falls in the birth rate.

iv If you change your politics you might find your circle of friends changes too. As people's level of income changes you often find their politics and their circle of friends change too.

c Writing scenarios

Students work in pairs. Assign scenarios to pairs according to the size of the group and to personal interests. Encourage the free play of imagination and give the pairs plenty of time to consider their scenarios. If they experience difficulty in thinking of scenarios, give them examples from the list of possible scenarios below.

Notes on vocabulary

Personal transport can mean cars, one-man helicopters, small 'cheap' microlight aircraft etc. *Communication technology* could refer to phones, videophones, computer networks, data banks etc.

Possible scenarios (examples only)

i Oil begins to run out – Petrol becomes impossibly expensive – Much more efficient electric batteries are developed – Cheap small electric cars become common.

ii Cordless phones become normal – Cheap pocket-sized videophones are produced – Most adults wear small videophones on their wrists as we now wear wrist-watches.

iii Many more countries have nuclear weapons – Two neighbouring client states of the superpowers come into (conventional) conflict – The country with the weaker conventional forces attacks the other with nuclear missiles despite the advice of its 'protecting' superpower – First the neighbouring states and then the superpowers themselves are drawn into the conflict.

iv Unemployment figures continue to increase – The government forces employers to introduce a shorter working week and more part-time work and job-sharing – The situation is reached where most working adults do not have a full-time job in the present sense.

v Replacement surgery becomes much more advanced – It becomes normal to replace hearts, livers, lungs and even brains – It becomes common to live to 150, most people dying not from disease but from accidents a long way from hospitals.

3   REPRESENTING RELATIONS

Students work as a group.

a
Possible answers

i   a breakdown
ii   a line graph
iii   a flow chart or a modified hierarchy
iv   a hierarchy
v   a pie chart
vi   a flow chart

b
Possible answers

i   flow chart
ii   a block graph
iii   a hierarchy
iv   a block graph
v   a pie chart
vi   a modified hierarchy or tree
vii   a pie chart

c
Possible answers

i   A line graph might be used to show numbers of students over the last twenty years; a *block graph* might be used to compare the number of first-class degrees in the different faculties; a *pie chart* might be used to represent the relative size of the various faculties; a *hierarchy* could be used to show the line of command among university officers; a *flow chart* would illustrate the way academic applications are processed; a *breakdown* might show the various sources of university finance (government grants, private endowments etc.); a *modified hierarchy or 'tree'* might show the administrative structure and general composition of the university.

ii   A *line graph* could be used to show production over the last five years; a *block graph* might show the company's sales in comparison with those of its five most important competitors; a *pie chart* could provide a breakdown of expenditure on research and development, salaries, production costs etc. A *hierarchy* could reflect the different grades of administrative staff; a *flow chart* could be used to display the production process; a *breakdown* would show the variety of fields the company is involved in; a *modified hierarchy or 'tree'* could be used to display the company structure.

4   READING THE SIGNS

a

Students work as a group. The exact definition of 'together' (i) could become part of the discussion: it could mean that they are a 'couple' or merely that for some reason they are having to spend some time together (e.g. a secretary having to 'look after' a visitor to the company).

Encourage discussion by raising objections to the students' conclusions:

i   But they might have just had a row?

ii   They might be *older* but how do we know they're more senior? OK, he's got a *bigger* desk, but it's in the worst *position*.

iii   But age doesn't come into it – he might be a mature student.

Answers

i   No, they are total strangers.

ii   The second and third from the left.

iii   The woman, third from right.

b   Letting people know

Students work in pairs. Assign (i)–(v) to pairs according to numbers. In (ii) assume that the couple are in a group at, for example, a party.

Possible answers

i   We give them a lot of eye-contact and smile at them; we face them for relatively longer than the other members; when several people are talking or trying to talk at the same time we favour those in whom we are interested.

ii   We sit or stand very close, perhaps touching; we give them a lot of eye-contact; if we are sitting our knees might face inwards towards them and theirs towards us; occasionally we might talk to each other in a much lower voice than is used for contact with outsiders.

iii   We look round as if hoping to find someone else to talk to; we try to let the conversation drop by not responding to what he or she says and failing to give the normal signs of agreement (e.g. nodding, sympathetic eye-contact).

iv   We give a great deal of eye-contact, and signs of agreement; we perhaps sit or stand quite close in particular with our head relatively close to theirs, often facing downwards.

v   We look attentively at the speaker and adopt a thoughtful expression; we nod occasionally as if gratefully appreciating the full implication of what has just been said; we smile or laugh at any witticism whether or not we find it funny.

Suggested supplementary questions

Do these (often insincere) messages we send out really matter? What happens if we don't bother with them?

Further possibility

Obviously this section gives an excellent opportunity for role-play, with students acting out the situations in (i)–(v). This would provide them with more data to supplement their answers.

2   Students work as a group. After checking that they know the vocabulary, elicit examples of (i)–(vii) from the students and then consider the answers to (2). Remind students that there are often several possibilities for each.

Possible answers

i   tiredness, boredom, romantic involvement, exasperation
ii   tiredness, boredom
iii   irritation, anger
iv   assent, confirmation
v   complicity (e.g. trying to get someone to keep quiet about a certain subject when in a group of people talking together)
vi   disapproval, perplexity
vii   impolite curiosity, anger

c   What's happened?

Students work as a group.

Possible answers

i   Somebody must have told him a joke.
ii   Somebody's said something to him that he doesn't like; somebody's insulted / offended him.
iii   They've just disagreed about something.
iv   He must have seen something very frightening – perhaps a large dangerous snake.

5   OLD-FASHIONED LOGIC

Students work as a group.

Notes

The figures relate to pre-1971 currency (12 old pence = 1 shilling; 20 shillings = £1). In 1971, the UK changed to its present decimal currency (100 pence = £1). 20 shillings (=£1) was a low wage seventy years ago. 1/3 (one shilling and threepence) was $\frac{1}{16}$ of £1.

Here is how Alan Brownjohn himself describes how the poem came to be written: '"Common Sense" was compiled, or assembled – rather than written – after browsing through some problems in an old arithmetic manual. I noticed how the little stories told in presenting the problems contained an interesting commentary on the period in which they were written. The last stanza comes from the preface to the manual.'

Suggested supplementary questions

Stanza 1:   What proportion of your salary would you expect to spend on food?
Stanza 2:   In what area of employment are fines accepted (e.g. professional sport)?
Stanza 7:   Which part of the world is suggested? (Africa? India?)

Possible answers (examples only)

Stanza 1: That life on the land was very hard.
Stanza 2: The degree of social control was greater than now.
Stanza 3: That there were no strictly enforced regulations regarding the composition of milk as there are now.
Stanza 4: That people who were unable to support themselves financially were almost a separate social class.
Stanza 5: That very high casualties were considered 'normal'.
Stanza 6: That education was the key to social advancement.
Stanza 7: That sieges in foreign countries with perhaps hostile climates (18 miles per day is not very much) were common experiences during the time of the Empire.

6   ARGUMENTATION BY IMAGES

Students work as a group.

Notes

The first photograph is of a football crowd at Ellis Park, Johannesburg, and the second is of a priest of the Verona Fathers holding the hand of a starving Karamojong boy in Uganda.

C LISTENING ACTIVITIES

The *theme* is experience of what may be considered to be logical. The *objective* is to facilitate natural discussion and shared activity. The activity has three parts.

Listening activity 1 may seem very easy, but it can generate a great deal of discussion.

In activity 2, do insist on students hearing this only once. All instructions are included in the tapescript. The objective is to create stress and play on students' expectation. Please insist on the time limit.

The teacher should try to be straight-faced and refuse to divulge information or give help.

1
Suggested answers

a   Open. 'He was the first person the man met.' 'Policemen are authority figures.'
b   Open.
c   The policeman didn't realise that the chimpanzee was being entertained, was considered to be a friend.
d   'Do you think I should?'
e   Is it my duty? My obligation? What would be best for the chimp?

2
Suggested answers

a   Open. Possibilities are a set of weights, dumb-bells, balloon captions.
b   Students were never asked to write. The final instruction was to *print*.

Tapescript

1

A man was walking along with a chimpanzee on a lead when he saw a policeman. 'Excuse me, Constable,' he said. 'Where do you think I should take this chimp?' 'Why don't you take him to the zoo?' suggested the policeman.

The following day, the same man bumped into the same policeman. 'I thought you were taking that chimp to the zoo,' remarked the constable. 'I did just that, thank you', replied the man. 'But he likes a change, so today I'm taking him to the cinema.'

2

a   You will now be asked to follow some simple instructions, which will be heard only once. You will need paper and pen or pencil. Now listen carefully.

  i   Draw a circle approximately the same size as the largest coin in your country.
  ii   Now draw an identical circle two inches to the right of the first circle.
  iii Join the two circles with a straight line.
       Give a name to the object you have drawn.

b   You will now hear a second more difficult set of instructions. Do not write anything until you are told to do so. Ready?

  i   What is the capital of Paraguay?
  ii   How many countries are contained in the continent of Africa?
  iii Who discovered penicillin?
  iv   What is the main export of Venezuela?
  v   How long has the EEC been in existence?
  vi   Now print your surname.

D STRUCTURE AND LANGUAGE USAGE

Students work as a group. Do (1)–(4) as a 'round-the-class' exercise.

1

Possible answers

a

  i   Sorry, I didn't intend to do that.
  ii   Sorry, I didn't do that deliberately.
  iii Sorry, that wasn't intentional.

b

  i   This will make it necessary to cut down on expenditure all round.
  ii   This will mean cutting down on expenditure all round.
  iii This will involve cutting down on expenditure all round.

c

  i   To this day the police have discovered/found no explanation for the crime.
  ii   To this day the police have no idea of the motive for the crime./To this day the police have found/discovered no motive for the crime.

d

   i   Our target is a £3 million turnover this year.
   ii   We're trying to achieve a £3 million turnover this year./We want to achieve a . . .
   iii We're aiming at a £3 million turnover this year./We aim to have a . . ./We're aiming to have . . .

e

   i   What effect will these changes have on our company?
   ii   What will the consequences of these changes be for our company?/What consequences will these changes have for our company?

f

   i   What's the purpose of/behind all these meetings?
   ii   What's the reason for all these meetings?

g

   i   These attitudes seem to shape a lot of her thoughts and actions.
   ii   These attitudes seem to lie behind a lot of her thoughts and actions.

2

Possible answers

a   What's the point in doing it? – There's no incentive.
b   I don't want to seem cynical, but what is his ulterior motive?
c   his students seem to lack any motivation.
d   I don't quite understand how he reaches these/those/his conclusions.
e   I've achieved all my goals in life.

3   *If . . .*

Possible answers (examples only)

a   Jim's wife thinks that if Jim hadn't missed his train and been 45 minutes late for the interview he would/might have got the job.
b   Jim, however, thinks he might have got the job if he hadn't been so argumentative.
c   He would have been offered the job if he hadn't lacked experience with the latest technology . . .
d   Some historians maintain that if President Kennedy hadn't been assassinated, he would have become unpopular as a result of US involvement in Vietnam.
e   If, seventy years ago, ships' radios had been manned 24 hours a day, the Titanic's distress signals would have been picked up.
f   If there hadn't been unusually low temperatures immediately before the launch, the 1986 Challenger space-shuttle disaster would not have occurred.
g   If the rubber seals on the booster rockets hadn't been damaged/a fuel leak would not have occurred/there would not have been a fuel leak.
h   If he had been given more encouragement to follow the career of his choice, he would not have wasted several years in the wrong job.
i   If he hadn't said what he did, he might not have been found guilty./If he hadn't committed the crime, he wouldn't have said what he did./If he hadn't lost his temper, he wouldn't have said what he did.

4

Possible answers

a

    i   . . . have been eroded, resulting in a general rebellion against . . .

    ii   . . . have been eroded and as a consequence there has been a general rebellion against established values.

    iii   The erosion of the traditional social disciplines has led to a general . . .

    iv   The traditional social disciplines having been eroded, there has been a general rebellion . . .

b

    i   If we fail to regenerate the largely self-enforcing social and moral disciplines, the argument for repression will gain acceptance.

    ii   Unless we regenerate the largely self-enforcing social and moral disciplines, the argument . . .

    iii   We must regenerate the largely self-enforcing social and moral disciplines (in order) to prevent acceptance of the argument for repression.

    iv   We must regenerate the largely self-enforcing social and moral disciplines in case the argument for repression gains acceptance.

c

    i   Seeing that the standards of state education have fallen in recent years, we're saving up to give our children a private education.

    ii   Standards of state education having fallen in recent years, we're saving up to give our children a private education.

    iii   The reason we're saving up to give our children a private education is that the standards of state education have fallen in recent years.

E WRITING ACTIVITY

1   (READING TEXT A)

b

Possible answers (examples only)

    i   . . . identify the causes.

    ii   . . . we can find remedies.

    iii   . . . led to/brought about a great improvement in matters of public health.

    iv   . . . a reversal of these trends; . . . the/an erosion of social disciplines.

    v   . . . have simple rules to live by they very easily become brutalised; . . . have a framework of social discipline they very easily become brutalised.

    vi   . . . we need to/must regenerate the largely self-enforcing social and moral disciplines; . . . we must turn our minds towards regenerating . . .

    vii   reliance on repressive disciplines will almost certainly gain credence as a lesser evil.

    viii . . . self-enforcing social and moral disciplines must be regenerated.

2   APHORISMS AND PROVERBS

Possible answers

i   If you know what somebody is like when they are very young, you can predict what they will be like as adults.

ii   At 25 it's easy to be talented, but if you're 50 it's much more difficult.

iii   If you're happy, everybody wants to share your happiness, but if you're unhappy they don't want to get involved (or 'they don't want to know' (colloquial)).

iv   If you want to lead men, you have to keep your distance from them.

v   If you are great, you are able to make opportunities.

vi   If there are rumours about something, there's probably a good reason for them.

vii   If you are not perfect yourself, don't criticise other people for not being so.

3A   EXTENSION TEXT COMPLETION

Possible answer

In the mid-eighteenth century the interaction of social, scientific and economic developments **brought about/created/caused** conditions that **led** to/were conducive to the occurrence of what we now call 'The Industrial Revolution': labour resources had been **created** by the changing patterns of agricultural production and ownership of the land **so that** opportunities for work in the new Northern towns immediately **caused** an influx of job-seekers from both the country and Ireland.

Recently invented textile machinery **associated** with such names as Arkwright **necessitated** that factories be built **to/in order to** house them. But there was a price to pay for this development: insanitary conditions and over-crowding in these jerry-built towns **led to/bred/caused** disease, deprivation and social conflict.

4 OMISSION

Themes	Reformers, human failings, avoiding responsibility, regrets, deprivation
Functions	Discussing human failings, expressing dislikes, expressing regret, suggesting remedies
Structures	Ellipsis. 'Wish' and 'if only' structures, Should, need. Passives (with and without 'get'). Passive gerund. Verb patterns: need, forget, omit, fail, regret, bother.
Phonology	Weak and strong forms

Examples: **Weak**	**Strong**
☐	☐
He lives down the road.	He talks down to me.
☐	☐
She takes me for granted.	What's it for?

Conditionals. Rhythm and stress.

☐	
I wish I'd been with you.	(I'm sorry I wasn't)
☐	
I wish I'd been with you.	(I didn't like the person I was with.)
☐	
I wish I'd been with you.	(Even if you don't)
☐ ☐	☐ ☐
If only I'd known.	(But I didn't)

Intonation in reduced utterances.
Final rising intonation in yes/no type questions.
(Did you) go into town?
(Would you) like a chocolate?
Final falling intonation in imperatives.
(I hope you) have a good trip.
(Do) enjoy yourself.

Lexis	lack (v + n), shortage, absence, short (of), could do with, fall short of expectations, shortfall, not very good at, to be snubbed, to be passed over, to be taken for granted, to be patronised, to be stood up, to be talked down to, to be kept in the dark, to be manipulated

A READING TEXTS

1 READING

The Bradbury text is longer than the extract from Hazlitt, but the latter is appreciably more difficult because of its denser texture and greater age.

Notes on Text A

Warn students that this is not a contemporary text and that they will encounter some archaic or less current vocabulary or structure. They should *not* worry if they do not understand every word.

din and smithery = noise and fuss.
practique = practical.
theorique = theoretical.
cudgel = a stick or club.
not hung up in monumental mockery = full of archaisms, dead

2 QUESTIONS ON THE TEXTS

Suggested supplementary questions

Supplementary to Question (b): Is it later than Shakespeare? Which century does it come from? Which authors writing in English in 18th or 19th century have you read? Is it earlier or later than that? Is it before or after Dickens? *Answer*: Slightly less than 200 years ago.

Notes on Text B

In answering questions (a) and (b) on the text it may be useful to draw attention to some of the vocabulary: e.g. graveyard, tomblike, phantom, hawk, scarab-beetle (or dung beetle), museum specimen.

Suggested supplementary questions

Supplementary to Questions (a) and (c) on Text B: (But) What about the absence of crime?
Supplementary to Questions (b) on both texts: Wouldn't people's fear of the unorthodox, their conformism and their suspicion of the stranger be very similar?

B COMMUNICATIVE ACTIVITIES

1 IMPROVING CONDITIONS

Students work in pairs.

a   Steer students towards topics that are of particular interest to them such as health, the position of women, the constitution.

If you had been living in 1870 and working in a factory, what do you think life would have been like? Imagine that you were very poor and living a century ago, which social problems might you have experienced? What would have happened if you had been very poor and seriously ill for a long period?

b   Students work as a group.

c   Students work as a group.

Suggested supplementary questions

What do they seek to achieve and how do they operate? What means of persuasion do they use? What kinds of people or institutions might be involved? Who might use the (pejorative) terms 'busybodies' or 'do-gooders'?

d   Students work as a group.

Possible answers

Religious feelings/a feeling of duty/political belief/love of humankind.

e   Students work as a group.

2   WHAT'S THE PROBLEM? WHAT'S MISSING?

a   Students work in pairs. Encourage students to answer in full sentences wherever possible and to offer several alternative descriptions of the problem, followed where possible by a potential remedy. Perhaps there is no remedy in the case of (vi)?

i   She lacks (moral) courage; She lacks 'character'; She's too concerned about security; She should pluck up courage and tell him.

ii   There's no real communication between them; They don't talk to each other enough; There isn't enough closeness or sharing; He doesn't think enough about the effect of these matters on his wife.

iii   He makes no attempt to understand her; He's rather insensitive to her feelings; He should talk to her more; He ignores her feelings and anxieties; He should try to take her feelings more seriously.

iv   They have a lack of feeling for the needs of employees; There's inadequate consultation; They should take their employees into their confidence.

v   They don't show any consideration for others; They're selfish and inconsiderate; They should think about other people a bit more.

vi   He shows no remorse; He doesn't feel ashamed of what he has done.

vii   He isn't very good at managing meetings; He's rather short on committee skills; He should go on a course to train him in chairing committees.

viii   They didn't do enough market research; They lacked business sense; They hadn't planned properly; They hadn't done enough homework; They should study market requirements more closely.

b   Students work in pairs.

i   Assign the items to different pairs. Give the pairs ample time to consider their answers and encourage them to give detailed examples.

Possible answers (examples only)

i   You have a disagreement on the phone with somebody close; they put the phone down mid-conversation.
ii You're at a party and somebody who knows you behaves as if you are a stranger.
iii There is a possibility of promotion at work and in the normal course of events you could expect to get it but you don't.
iv Your daughter and son-in-law always assume you will be available without notice for baby-sitting on Saturday nights; at work you feel your skills and willingness for example to do after-hours work are no longer properly rewarded.
v   When the Chairman of the Company visits he always asks the most irritating questions and makes everybody feel as if they are his servants.
vi At work colleagues try to get you to do or say certain things in order to help their interests.
vii A work associate you trusted has failed to keep a promise.
viii You arrange a romantic meeting with a member of the opposite sex but they don't turn up.
ix You know quite a lot about computers but a computer engineer you deal with treats you as if you are a beginner.
x   The workforce are not told about impending changes in the ownership of the company. The employees first hear about it on television.

ii

Possible answers

i   self-control; good manners
ii   no answer possible
iii recognition for what they have done; the right qualifications; 'a face that fits'
iv   realization of how much the person does or contributes
v   respect; sensitivity
vi   no answer possible
vii reliability; dependability
viii consideration
ix   humility; sensitivity
x   consultation; communication

c   Students work in pairs.

3   IF ONLY . . .

Students work as a group.

Suggested supplementary questions

Supplementary to (b) and (c): Isn't it better to err on the side of security and caution?
Supplementary to (d): 'Wouldn't you have liked to have become a . . .' 'Isn't there any other job you would have rather done?'

4   MAKE IT SNAPPY!

a   Students work as a group.

Possible answers

i   Removal services
ii   Car hire; catering services; a hotel
iii   throat tablets/lozenges; a gargle
iv   a pension fund; a building society; an international estate agency
v   a corporation (trying to attract companies to its area); a commercial estate agency
vi   a garage (offering to put your car through the official annual test of roadworthiness)

b

Possible answers

i   Do-it-yourself holidays (offering flight only with a minimum of help with accommodation); a package holiday to a new holiday destination. Reducible to: *Tired of package holidays*?
ii   A company offering financial services; a pension fund. Reducible to: *Totally satisfied with your pension arrangements*?
iii   A finance company; a bank offering long-term loans. Reducible to: *Having difficulty balancing your budget*?
iv   A tax adviser; an accountancy firm; the tax department of a bank. Reducible to: *Worried about your tax*?
v   A holiday firm specialising in short breaks (e.g. a four-day trip to Austria); a hotel offering reduced weekend rates. Reducible to: *Feel like a break*?

c   Students work as a group. Students should be made aware of the fact that the reduced forms tend to be more informal. This is very clear in (vii) in particular.
         Note that all except (viii) and (ix) are questions requiring 'yes/no' answers and end with rising intonation.

Possible answers

i·   Go into town?
ii   Like a cigarette?/Cigarette?
iii   Sleep well?
iv   Lot of traffic?
v   Got change for £10?
vi   Like a chocolate?/Chocolate?
vii   Got the time?
viii   Another piece of cake?
ix   Have a good trip!
x   Ready?

5   PRIVATION

'Untouchable' also means a Hindu of very low caste. The 'fists' are those of prison officers or other inmates. The 'paws' are those of prison officers carrying out body searches.

Suggested supplementary questions

Supplementary to question (a): What are the 'patting paws' and 'the indifferent probing away'? Why does the author say 'I want to want to be touched'?

C LISTENING ACTIVITIES

The *theme* is what is not said and is meant to be understood. The *objective* is to make students more aware of abbreviated utterances and their implications.

The activity should allow freedom of interpretation based on verbal content and intonation. The teacher may feel forced to explain certain colloquial expressions, such as: 'where in the world'; 'you know how it is'; 'I can't make it'; 'something's come up'. However, these expressions are simply providing an authentic background and should not be allowed to take over the lesson. Concentrate on the students' activities and attempt to monitor their analyses.

1

Possible answers

Dialogue a

i	Mr Long appears to be superior/the boss.
ii	There are key words to indicate that the scene took place just before Christmas.
iii	Mr Long seems to feel that Miss B. is just having a day off.
iv	We do not *know* exactly what has happened.

Dialogue b

i	Apparently very tentative.
ii	He was more involved with Clara than she was with him. He had been planning an engagement party.
iii	Open.

Dialogue c

i	He is worried about his health.
ii	He makes it clear that he thinks the problem is in the patient's mind.
iii	He feels rebuffed/he is too frightened to discover what the problem really is.

Dialogue d

i	A friend or acquaintance.
ii	Their jealousy because the lady has found a rich friend.
iii	There is something improper about the relationship.

Dialogue e

i	Obviously, they have very different expectations.
ii	The appraiser is reviewing past performance. The appraisee wants to look to the future.

Tapescript

There are five snatches of dialogue to follow. Students are asked to look for unsaid messages, hidden meanings.

a

Office man   Hello, hello. Is that Miss Bright? Where in the world are you, Miss Bright? I've had to let myself into the office. The heating wasn't switched on . . . no coffee waiting . . .

Miss B.   That's why I'm ringing, Mr Long. I can't get my car to start. I'll be in as soon as I can.

Office man	And when will that be?
Miss B.	I've rung the A.A. and someone will come right away, they say. But you know how it is. This time of year, so much traffic, everyone out doing last minute shopping, icy roads . . .
Office man	I take it that you won't be in today.

b

Clara	At last, Henry! I've been ringing you every night this week.
Henry	Can't understand why you haven't been able to get through. I've been here . . . a quiet week, in fact. Never mind. I'll be seeing you on Saturday.
Clara	That's just the thing, Henry. I'm afraid I can't make it. Something's come up and there's no way of getting out of it. I was sure you would understand.
Henry	(*stunned pause*) But, Clara . . . You know as well as I do that this wasn't a run-of-the mill meeting. I've been to the jewellers and . . . I've said goodbye to Jane. Not to mention the mortgage we've discussed . . . and the tickets for the Royal Ballet.
Clara	Ring you back, Henry. There's someone at the door.

c

Patient	Doctor, this pain in my chest doesn't seem to be getting any better. My wife's getting impatient. Says I'm putting it on. And the boss is none too pleased either.
Doctor	So you're finding problems at home and at work. What is it that you would like me to do? I'm not a counsellor, you know. Far too busy with measles and mumps and bronchitis and arthritis . . .
Patient	Yes, you're a busy man. Could you write out a repeat prescription for the pain-killers, please?

d

Mavis	I'm not one to gossip, but . . . have you seen her new car? Can't imagine how she can afford to run it . . . a big car like that.
Doris	She doesn't have to pay, does she? Not like us. Clean, decent, hard-working women and we have to queue for buses.
Mavis	Shouldn't be too hard on her, dear. She's had a hard life. Buried two husbands and brought up six children. Still, that's no reason to depart from the straight and narrow path.
Doris	You're right. Mustn't pass judgement. But I still think it's wrong to take advantage of an old man's weakness.

e

Appraiser	Thank you for coming, Peter. Are you quite clear about the reason for our appraisal meeting?
Appraisee	Well, not entirely clear. I suppose it's about that business of the tribunal.
Appraiser	Not really, that is to say not entirely. We are meant to be discussing your job performance and your hopes for the future. That has been made very clear to me at a recent management course.
Appraisee	Mmmh . . . management course. Now that is one thing I've been thinking about. I'm quite sure that I could do a better job if I had some up-to-date training.
Appraiser	Interesting that you should have brought up the matter of that unfortunate tribunal. (*riffling through papers*) Lost the case, I see.
Appraisee	Yes, but I thought you said that . . .

D STRUCTURE AND LANGUAGE USAGE

1

Students work in pairs. As there are a lot of very important structural items in this paraphrasing exercise, not all of which have come up in the earlier sections of this unit, it is particularly important that students should prepare for it by working through the Study Notes.

An important implicit contrast in this exercise is that between 'I needn't have done it' (= I did it unnecessarily) and 'I didn't need to do it' (= I didn't do it because it was unnecessary). The former meaning is suggested by the use of 'waste' in (h) and (k).

If necessary, give students the first word of the possible answer.

Possible answers (examples only)

a

i	The Board wish they had diversified two or three years ago.
ii	The Board regret not diversifying two or three years ago.

b

i	Jane feels she should have done a different subject at university.
ii	Jane wishes she had done a different . . .

c

i	If only I'd worked harder at maths.
ii	I regret not working harder at maths.

d

i, ii, iii   The engineer failed/forgot/omitted to check the pressure gauge.

e

i	There's a need for more maths teachers.
ii	There's a shortage of maths teachers.

f

i	I needn't come along, need I?; I don't need to come along, do I?
ii	It isn't necessary for me to come along, is it?

g

i	There's a lack of understanding among the people at the top.
ii	There's an absence of understanding on the part of the people at the top.

h

i	We needn't have gone.
ii	It wasn't necessary for us to go.

i

i	Both companies have had/experienced a shortfall in orders.
ii	Orders have fallen short of both companies' expectations.

j

i	We're short of two chairs.
ii	We're two chairs short.

k

   i   I needn't have written to him because I saw him the next day.

   ii   I needn't have bothered to write to him because I saw him the next day.

l

   i   His hair needs cutting.

   ii   His hair could do with a cut; He could do with a haircut.

m

   i   He lacks any idea about how to manage people.

   ii   He's no good at managing people; He isn't any good at managing people.

2

Students work in pairs

Possible answers

a   Those responsible (for this) will be punished.

b   While in Cairo he started learning conversational Arabic.

c   The government ministers involved in these tax scandals were forced to resign.

d   This substance, discovered entirely by accident, later proved to be a hitherto unknown element.

e   He stared at the floor, too nervous to reply.

f   Although already middle-aged, she was still strikingly beautiful.

g   Whether true or untrue, it shouldn't have been said.

h   The poor and (the) sick from the surrounding area used to come to them for help.

i   His last request, for his son to visit him, was never met./His last request, that his son should visit him, was never met.

j   On the way up the drive, Watson happened to notice a man half hidden by the tall bushes.

k   The main argument of his school of thought, that scientific laws have no exceptions, was unacceptable to contemporaries.

3   PASSING THE BUCK

Students work in pairs. Insist that students produce a whole sentence and also that they suggest several alternatives wherever possible. Give prompts only if absolutely necessary.

Possible answers

a

   i   We broke all the glasses.

   ii   Employees have been taking things home from the office; You've been stealing things from the office.

   iii   I dropped it; I let go of it.

   iv   I was going too fast; I didn't brake early enough.

   v   I didn't see him come out; I was looking at something on the other side and didn't see him; I was travelling much too fast.

   vi   I've overspent; I haven't budgeted very well.

   vii   I don't know how to operate this machine; I can't operate this machine.

   viii   I threw it away; You threw it away, didn't you?

   ix   I've put it somewhere silly/in the wrong place.

b

i Somehow the wrong batteries got put in; The wrong batteries were put in somehow.
ii This Volkswagen suddenly came out from nowhere/without warning.
iii The money's running out/going out too quickly/not going to last.
iv The whole character of the place has been changed.
v Somehow all the invoices had got mixed up, causing chaos in the Accounts Office.
vi Some envelopes and quite a lot of stamps have gone missing. (colloquial)
vii The whole problem's got confused now.

E WRITING ACTIVITIES

2
Possible answer

'An Iranian plane crashed in south-western Iran on Friday. Iran's official news agency said the transport came down just before landing owing to technical failure. The C-130/Hercules was carrying 91 soldiers and 7 crew when it smashed into/hit the side of one of the highest mountains in the area.'

5 THE GENERAL AND THE PARTICULAR

Themes	The qualities of the teacher, the problems of secondary-school teaching, the state and the individual, assertiveness training, stereotypes and generalisations
Functions	Talking about 'the ideal', talking about the rights and duties of the individual. Stating how you want to be treated by others, focusing attention
Structures	Collective nouns; particularisers; ought to, should, must, supposed to; irregular plurals; plurals of foreign words; plurals of compounds □ □ □
Phonology	Syllable stress; shift (technique, technical, technicality)
Lexis	□ □

generalise, exemplify, illustrate, peculiar to, peculiarity, characteristic of, detail, specifics, idea, technicality, generalities, outline, minutiae, general terms, gist, itemise, specify, applicable, incorporate, merge, swallow up, assimilate, integrate, become part of, in particular, primarily, notably, principally, specifically, specially, mostly, mainly, chiefly, largely, solely, simply, alone, exclusively

A READING TEXTS

2   QUESTIONS ON THE TEXTS

Text A

Suggested supplementary question

Is it possible that the ideal of a teacher described by John Holt is out of date and inappropriate now?

Both texts

Guide students towards a discussion of those topics that most concern them and consider education in the widest sense, from the provision of crêches or nursery school places to grants for university research.

B   COMMUNICATIVE ACTIVITIES

1   IDEALS AND ACTUALITIES

Students work as a group.

Suggested supplementary questions

a   What should a police officer be like ideally? Imagine the perfect politician: what would he or she be like?

Possible answers

i   Fair, unprejudiced, calm, incorruptible. Made difficult by distrust of and aggression towards police.
ii   Disinterested servants of the community. Honourable and statesmanlike. Incorruptible. Electors want image rather than character. The selection processes often favour the wrong people.
iii   Hardworking, with wide intellectual and cultural interests (not just in their own subject).

b

Suggested supplementary questions

How would you rate yourself as a student in the eyes of (a) your teachers? (b) your fellow students? (c) your family? (d) yourself? Why do you think you fall short of your ideal, if you do?

c

Possible answers (examples only)

That I'll do an hour's jogging a day; that I'll eat more fibre and less salt; that I'll be a less selfish person.

What prevents you keeping to it? Why do you find it so difficult?

d   Add local examples where appropriate: for example there may be a system that depends on the honesty of the individual, such as the use of a photocopier or a telephone which has a book beside it for individuals to record their use in.

Suggested supplementary questions

Are you absolutely sure you would always . . .? But don't you think you ought to mention it? Shouldn't you bring it to his/her notice? Shouldn't you say something?

2   THE STATE AND THE INDIVIDUAL

Students work as a group.

Conscientious objectors (ix) are people who gain exemption from military service on grounds of pacifist beliefs. In the UK they have been required to work on the land, in hospitals or, in time of war, in the factories involved in the war effort.

Suggested supplementary questions

(Note that (i), (iii), (vi), (ix) and (x) should be adjusted to fit local circumstances.)

i   How much help has the individual the right to expect from the state?
ii   What does the individual owe to the state?
iii   How many years of military service has the state the right to ask for?
iv   Has it got anything to do with the state? Isn't it just a private matter?
v   Is it a duty? But how can a 'feeling' be a 'duty'? Either you have the feeling or you don't?
vi   What happens when this freedom is absent? What happened in this connection in the history of this country?
vii   What about the influence of money on the law?
viii   (The UK constitution is unwritten.) Should a constitution be written or unwritten? What should it contain? What does ours contain?
ix   Should they be allowed to avoid what others have to endure? Should they have to prove that their pacifism comes from religious belief? Should we allow people to be conscientious objectors?
x   What about people or institutions that abuse freedom of speech, for example magazines and newspapers that fabricate interviews and publish lies about people?

Possible answers

i   Everybody contributes to it compulsorily through taxation and in return has the right to, for example, free education for their children, free medical care, and financial assistance in the event of hardship.
ii   Every citizen is required to pay taxes in return for services provided by the state.
iii   Citizens have a duty to do military service for their country if and when required.
iv   We owe it to our country to bring up the next generation (of citizens). It's our own private decision/It's nothing to do with the state.
v   It's love for our country. A feeling of loving and belonging.
vi   The right to worship as we please/want to without being persecuted.
vii   When everyone is equal under/in the eyes of/the law. No one is above the law. The law applies equally to everyone (irrespective of rank/position/status).

viii The embodiment of the principles and laws of a nation where the basic rights of the individual are set down (in the case of a written constitution like that of the US).

ix The right of an individual to refuse to do combat service if it is against his conscience/religious beliefs/religion to do so.

x The right of people to express opinion/debate freely. The right of newspapers to publish without censorship.

b Encourage discussion of new topics, e.g. being a good representative abroad. Enhancing your country's reputation abroad. Helping your country build a better future?

c

Possible answers

Law and order. Good social services. Efficient administration. Defence against the country's enemies.

d

Suggested supplementary question

Where do we/should we draw the line between the community's desire for order and the individual's desire for freedom?

Possible answer

Perhaps at the point where the individual's freedom begins to restrict the freedom of others. (For example playing transistor radios in gardens or on the beach.)

This discussion could consider the following: washing or repairing cars in the street, parties in blocks of flats, laws against putting washing out to dry on Sunday (as in some parts of West Germany).

e

v welfare scroungers = a derogatory term for people who try to get as much financial help as possible from the state.

Suggested supplementary question

i, ii, iii Does the end ever justify the means?

3 THE INDIVIDUAL VERSUS THE REST

Students work as a group.

a Give students plenty of time to study the four types and to work out the meanings of any vocabulary they find difficult ('to con' is a colloquial expression meaning to deceive, cheat, or manipulate people).

Possible answers

d Loneliness? Resentfulness? Difficult relationships.

f Some feminists have maintained that too many women have fallen into the pattern of (iii) and need to learn assertiveness to avoid being exploited by a male-dominated society.

4   GENERALISATIONS

Students work as a group.

a   *Stereotypes*

Suggested supplementary questions

i   What kind of character is portrayed? What details of the drawing communicate that character?

ii   What would you say his attitude to life was? What about his walk? Which details particularly express the stereotype?

iii What's the significance of the smile? Would you expect it to be coffee or tea? (Probably tea.) What about the pipe?

iv   What would you say his state of mind is? Which details are important to the stereotype?

Possible answers (examples only)

i   bossiness; a disciplinarian; 'a schoolmarm'

ii   mindless obedience; unable to think for himself

iii a benevolent attitude; kindly; avuncular

iv   total preoccupation; the state of being oblivious to the rest of the world.

v   – rather fat, cigar, camera, shorts
     – short hair, aggressive, always fighting
     – macho appearance, politically right-wing
     – slim and healthy-looking, perhaps tanned, sensitive, precise and considerate behaviour
     – straight hair, athletic build, touchy (colloquial), argues aggressively

vi   Encourage students to suggest additional factors if possible (e.g. accommodation).

Possible questions

What kind of man drives a Porsche? What do you think when you see a young man or woman with very close-cropped hair? What sort of person goes to _____ for a holiday? What sort of person goes camping? What kind of person might go on a birdwatching holiday?

b   *Sweeping generalisations*

These extracts are from a very humorous (and affectionate) book and are not to be taken too seriously.

5   BELONGING

Students work as a group, and they should do this in two parts:

1   Elicit answers to (a) in the Student's Book.

2   Widen the discussion, with the help of the suggested questions below, and answer question (b) in the Student's Book. Discuss the *feelings* that link member to member and members to the others of the community, crew etc.

a
 i A group of nuns outside their convent which itself is part of a religious order. The convent in the photograph belongs to the Order of St Mary of the Cross.
 ii A parade of Protestant loyalists in Northern Ireland, part of the Orange Order formed in 1795 and named after King William III of England, pledged to maintain the status of the Protestant Community in Northern Ireland. These parades are an important factor in the unrest in the province.
 iii The lifeboatmen of Penlee lifeboat crew founded in 1913 and supported by voluntary contributions. The lifeboatmen frequently risk their lives to save seamen but receive no salary.
 iv The schoolgirls are members of a girls' boarding school or public school. The school in the photograph is Roedean founded in 1885.
 v These veterans were members of different regiments in the 1914–18 war and are now taking part in a parade to commemorate their fallen comrades.

Suggested supplementary questions

 i What is it, do you think, that makes a young woman want to become a nun? What is her life dedicated to?
 ii How would you describe the feelings that link the members? Would it be better for their country if they didn't have these feelings?
 iii Remembering that lifeboatmen are not paid for their dangerous work, what is it, do you think, that motivates them?
 iv What range of feelings do we have about our schooldays?
 v What might you feel if you were in their situation?
 (One prominent UK politician has said he wishes he had died with all those friends who were killed in the First World War because he feels it was unfair that he should have survived.)

C LISTENING ACTIVITY

The theme is historical change and development as contrasted with the effect of such change on the particular individual. For example, in 1895, Marconi invented radio telegraphy. What individual effect has that had?

1 Keeping warm and fed were the main priorities, with little regard for household hygiene or home decoration. Opportunities to widen horizons were limited, even for those who could read. Many activities were, of necessity, limited to daylight hours.

2 The objective is to encourage specific listening comprehension in activity (a) and to develop and use the information gathered in activity (b). The whole activity is designed to encourage students in the skill of note-taking.
 The teacher will find it important to check students' notes for accuracy. After activity (a) has been completed, the tape should be played again to give an opportunity for interpretive listening. In activity (b) the focus should be on accuracy of interpretation and original thought. There should be no correction of pronunciation or grammar unless meaning is misinterpreted and clarification is

needed. However, the teacher will want to monitor and take note of individual difficulties, which should be corrected later.

a
Possible answers

i benefits: discovery of penicillin, rabies vaccine
ii disasters: first atom bomb detonated, nuclear tests

Please note that there could be disagreement on some items. For example, transcontinental telephone calls have made information more instantly accessible, but they have also helped to destroy the art of letter-writing. The first man on the moon could be seen to represent a great scientific stride, but the enormous funds needed to support this could have been used to better life on earth.

Tapescript

Presenter   It can be easy to find proverbs which support and justify almost any standpoint or behaviour. One such proverb is the subject of my talk to you today: a change is as good as a rest. At its best an over-generalisation. At its worst an empty and patronising comment. A comment of little consolation to the friend who has to paint his flat instead of having a holiday. This much-quoted proverb leads me to the subject of change. Is the word 'change' a synonym for 'progress' . . . 'development'? How does the general concept of change affect the particular individual? Let us look back over the years between 1894 and 1974 . . . and study the implications of some changes.

Voice 1   1895: Röntgen discovers X-rays. Marconi invents radio telegraphy. The Lumière brothers invent a motion-picture camera. Pasteur devises a rabies vaccine.

Voice 2   1915: First transcontinental telephone call, between New York and San Francisco. 1920: 22 million people die from influenza. 1922: Insulin is first administered to diabetic patients. 1924: $2\frac{1}{2}$ million radios in use in USA.

Voice 1   1942: Enrico Fermi splits the atom. 1943: Polio kills 1200 in the US, and cripples thousands more. 1945: Discovery of penicillin. First atomic bomb detonated.

Voice 2   1969: The first man steps on to the moon. 1974: India becomes the sixth nation to explode a nuclear device and loses 20,000 victims in a smallpox epidemic. The Tower of London and Houses of Parliament are bombed. Britain, France and China conduct nuclear tests.

Presenter   There we have the historical facts. I'll leave it to you to answer my questions . . . and reach your own conclusions.

D STRUCTURE AND LANGUAGE USAGE

Students work as a group.

1

Possible answers

a   . . . go into detail/specifics; get down to details/specifics; discuss specifics/details

b   . . . by the minutiae/detail(s)/technicalities

c   . . . give me the gist/outline; tell me in general terms

d   . . . generally/in general terms

e   . . . in general terms/outline; the gist of; the overall picture

f   . . . a rough idea/an idea (in general terms)

g   . . . on a technicality

h   . . . great/a lot of attention to detail

2

Possible answers

a

     i   The pattern discovered in one case-history will not necessarily be applicable generally/generally applicable.

     ii   It won't necessarily be possible to generalise from (the pattern discovered in) one case-history.

     iii   It won't necessarily be possible to make generalisations from (the pattern discovered in) one case-history.

b

     i   Could you provide us with a list, specifying the things you'll be needing?

     ii   Could you itemise the things you'll be needing? Could you provide us with a list itemising . . .

     iii   Could you list the things . . .?

c

     i   That's a very good illustration of exactly the kind of attitude I was describing.

     ii   That illustrates (very well) the kind of attitude I was describing (very well).

     iii   That exemplifies (very well) the kind of attitude I was describing (very well).

d

     i   This problem is a peculiarity of engines of this type and year.

     ii   This problem is (a) characteristic of engines of this type and year.

     iii   This problem is peculiar to engines of this type and year.

3

Possible answers

a   . . . (been) merged with/incorporated into/become part of

b   . . . he was swallowed up by; she merged with; he became part of

c   . . . that they have begun to assimilate; that they have become/been integrated d ... to integrate (it) into/to assimilate it with the rest of the company

e ... it's been swallowed up by the city; it's become part of Newcastle; it's (been) merged with Newcastle; it's become/been incorporated into Newcastle.

4 FOCUSING ATTENTION

Possible answers

a Our products are not selling, primarily because they're overpriced.

b There were several grounds for complaint, specifically poor service, unimaginative menus and overpriced telephone calls.

c We were unable to back it, principally because of the expense.

d We shall not be tendering for the contract chiefly because of the time-scale involved.

e The accident was (largely) attributable (largely) to negligence on the part of the two signalmen.

f The opening date is being put back principally (in order) to give the new cast time to settle in.

5 GENERAL OR PARTICULAR?

Students work in pairs.

It is of course impossible here to do any justice to the complex problem of articles. The purpose of the present exercise is more to demonstrate the need for concentrated study and practice than to offer easy answers.

It should be emphasised that in each example (ii) should be more specific relative to (i) but the degree and nature of that specificity may vary in each case.

If necessary, give prompts as to how to achieve that greater specificity: Can you relate it to a particular type of person/individual/place/time?

Possible answers (examples only)

a
  i no match for a fully grown bear.
  ii waiting to see you.

b
  i needs constant nourishment.
  ii of a man like Einstein is more complex than a hundred giant computers.

c
  i uses his hands as well as his eyes to observe.
  ii who lives at the other end of the village is coming too.

d
  i has played a major role in 20th century social change.
  ii taxied to the terminal buildings and stopped.

e
  i a relatively large brain compared with other animals of similar size.
  ii eaten some of your flowers.

f
  i is an inherently more flexible mode of transport than a fixed-wing aircraft.
  ii suddenly flew out of the sun and landed 100 yards away.

g

    i   is the time of day when the town really wakes up.

    ii   was warm and scented.

h

    i   a kind of disease in her opinion.

    ii   ruining community life in our part of London.

i

    i   are often partly responsible for their predicament.

    ii   of that area are given a lot of help by local churches.

j

    i   is innate, some scientists argue.

    ii   of the fineness and energy found in da Vinci is very rare indeed.

k

    i   often deride the faith and simplicity of the religious.

    ii   working in Moscow have discovered a new anti-malarial vaccine.

l

    i   needs a very efficient visual memory.

    ii   I know is just getting recognition after twenty years' work.

m

    i   needs constant, expert maintenance.

    ii   flew overhead just as we looked up.

n

    i   has probably given more service to humans than any other animal.

    ii   finished the race riderless.

o

    i   was first thought of by Leonardo da Vinci.

    ii   hit the mountainside during a rescue mission.

E WRITING ACTIVITIES

3 FOCUSING ATTENTION

Possible answers

a   I'm simply saying (that) it isn't a particularly new idea.

b   I'm going there specifically to consult one of the researchers.

c   I'm turning it down solely because of the absurdly low salary.

d   Should you turn it down on that account alone?

e   I suppose it is not/isn't simply on that account; I suppose it is not/isn't simply because of that.

f   As far as I'm concerned it's purely a matter of convenience.

g   They will be exclusively available at selected retail outlets.

h   Man cannot live solely/exclusively in physical terms.

4 DIFFICULT PLURALS

Answers

basis, bases

cactus, cacti

lay-by, lay-bys

hypothesis, hypotheses

hero, heroes

goose, geese

stratum, strata

diagnosis, diagnoses

criterion, criteria

woman doctor, women doctors

gin-and-tonic, gin-and-tonics

memorandum, memoranda

close-up, close-ups

radius, radiuses or radii

genus, genera

synopsis, synopses

assistant treasurer, assistant treasurers

curriculum, curricula (possibly 'curriculums')

passer-by, passers-by

analysis, analyses

veto, vetoes

medium, mediums or media

locus, loci

syllabus, syllabuses or syllabi

thesis, theses

stimulus, stimuli

mother-in-law, mothers-in-law

nucleus, nucleuses or nuclei

Preparation of Texts A and B should be set as homework before the next Unit is attempted.

6 STANDPOINT

Themes	Political opinion, prejudice and discrimination, appropriate language, aspects of the self, argument in poetry, postcards and posters
Functions	Expressing and reporting opinions, comparing ideologies, discussing and defining prejudices, making invitations, requests and enquiries, expressing approval, disapproval and indignation, irritation and perplexity
Structures	Might, should, ought, could, supposed to, need, 'are to', wish, must, have to, 'future perfect'

Phonology	Intonation to express attitudes. For example, a response such as 'Oh, yes', indicating agreement, boredom, understanding, anger or lack of understanding.
	    Difficult words: gauged (rhymed with paged), taxes, to knock.
	    Weak forms in modal verbs such as 'shouldn't have', 'needn't have', 'might have', 'could have'.

Lexis	In (our) view, we see it as . . ., in (our) opinion, as far as we are concerned, I regard it as . . ., point of view, the way (I) see it . . . Protest, condemn, denounce, object(v), revulsion, condemnation, applaud, disapprove, disagree, disagreement, critical, disparage, scornful, allow, take exception

B COMMUNICATIVE ACTIVITIES

1 POLITICAL BELIEFS AND ISSUES

a Students work in pairs. If possible, link these political labels to the appropriate local examples.

Possible answers

i conservative (right-wing)
ii radical
iii social democratic
iv right-wing (conservative)
v liberal

b Students work in pairs and then report to the group. Assign items to pairs.

Possible answers

(The following reflect the state of affairs in the UK and should obviously be adjusted to fit the local situation.)

i *Left*: high taxation to pay for generous social services.
Right: keep taxation down because it 'destroys incentive'.

ii *Left*: generous financial provision for state education; expansion of educational opportunities for all; the encouragement of 'progressive' ideas in education.
Right: The encouragement of 'traditional values' in education; value for money from centres of learning; scepticism about 'new ideas' in education.

iii *Left*: accountability of police forces to the community; cooperation between community and police; tendency to see crime as result of impoverished social environment; dislike of punishment.
Right: strong support for police and courts; belief in punishment as a deterrent; refusal to accept social deprivation as an 'excuse' for crime.

iv *Left*: belief that military expenditure should be kept to a minimum, sometimes combined with anti-nuclear policies.
Right: belief in paying for a high degree of military preparedness even at the expense of, for example, social programmes.

v *Left*: belief that vital services to the community such as electricity and water should be under community control and not a source of private profit.
Right: belief that privatisation increases efficiency and prevents, for example, nationalised industries being a drain on the public purse.

vi *Left*: belief in equality of the sexes and the possibility of advancing this with the help of legislation.
Right: traditional, 'a woman's place is in the home' attitudes; scepticism about changes in this area.

c Students work in pairs.

Possible answers

i Liberals might criticise right-wingers for being heartless/elitist/reactionary.
Right-wingers might criticise liberals for being 'soft' (on e.g. law and order)/too idealistic/unrealistic and with an exaggerated belief in human goodness.

ii Communists might criticise socialists for being 'half-hearted'/not being fully committed to the elimination of e.g. private property/believing in a gradual approach. Socialists might criticise communists for being totalitarian/authoritarian/anti-democratic.

iii Both these American political parties are relatively conservative/right-wing compared with their e.g. European counterparts. Republicans (US) might criticise Democrats for being 'soft' on law and order/for wasting money on 'welfare handouts'/for keeping taxes high. Democrats might criticize Republicans for making life easy for big business/looking after the rich/not doing enough for the disadvantaged/pursuing a narrowly self-interested foreign policy.

d Students work as a group.

Possible answers

i   By parents, education, friends, early experience.
ii   By age (people are said to become more conservative with age), general experience of life, by being *shocked* (e.g. by the famine in Ethiopia), by a personal loss of ideals.
iii By opinion-polls, by interviewing a representative cross-section of people.
iv   By the actual performance of the government you voted for, by political scandals.

e Students work as a group.

Possible answers

i   A sectional interest that tries systematically to influence public opinion in its favour.
ii   It believes in aggressive action in pursuit of its aims.
iii General agreement.
iv   Moderate, tending towards neither extreme.
v   Believing that a small section of the community is superior in its leadership qualities, judgement, intellectual ability etc.

Suggested supplementary question

How would the *opponents* of lobbies – *militant* unions, people who believe in getting a *consensus* before acting, *middle-of-the-roaders* and *elitists* – attack them? For example, they might say that lobbies distort the operation of a democracy.

2   PREJUDICE AND DISCRIMINATION

Students work as a group.

a

Other possible prejudices

against the old, against the opposite sex, against foreigners, against people from a different part of the country, against people who are more or less educated than you are

iii Students work in pairs. Examples: Do you have 'hippie'-types or punks in your country? Do you have any gypsies? Do you have immigrants from another continent? In the UK Northerners and Southerners are prejudiced about each other and make fun of the way the others talk. Some British people are prejudiced against politicians, teachers, male hairdressers, ballet dancers, accountants etc.

Are some regional dialects more 'acceptable' than others? Do people try to modify their dialect speech in favour of the 'standard' form of the language? Why do they do this?

b   vi   'Gays' are (generally male) homosexuals.

Possible answers

i   People think/there's 'something wrong with them'/that they ought to be married.
ii   People think they aren't as clean/hardworking/law-abiding as they are. They don't like their 'strange' food/customs.
iii   People treat them as if they are stupid and without normal feelings. They are treated like young children.
iv   They are often treated like rather difficult children. Their skills and experience are ignored.
v   They are considered to have a 'problem'. They are made fun of.
vi   (males) are considered weak and psychologically damaged.

d   Supplement the activity with local examples if possible.

Possible names

i   Sexism?
ii   Conformism? Intolerance?
iii   No special name
iv   Ageism?
v   Sexism? Male chauvinism?

e

Possible answers

It's taking things too far./It's being oversensitive. She's perfectly justified in bringing it to their attention.

Suggested supplementary question

Are minority groups ever right to object to certain language as discriminatory and 'part of the problem' or would it be over-sensitive to bother about it?

3   ADJUSTING OUR LANGUAGE OR PERSONALITY

Language

Students work in pairs and then report to group.

a   Get the students to think of *all* the people they might meet in the course of a morning, from the moment they open their eyes till lunchtime, and to consider how and why their greetings vary. For example, I might say 'Morning, darling' to my wife, 'Morning, Jim' to a colleague, 'Good Morning, Mr Jenks' to my boss. Similarly I might say 'Coffee?' or 'Like some coffee?', 'Would you like some coffee?' or 'Can I get you some coffee?' according to whether I was talking to a friend or an important professional visitor.

b

Possible answers

Degree of familiarity; professional relationship; age of participants; nature of request, enquiry or invitation (Because a lot of people don't like lending their car we might say '*Would you mind lending* me your car' to a very good friend, but '*Can I borrow* that paper-back you mentioned?')

c

Possible answers

i   Morning!

ii   Morning, Robert!/Hi! (colloquial)

iii   Good morning, Mr Li, did you have a good trip?

d

For example, invite somebody to the cinema, ask for some help with your suitcase, and ask the time. Vary them according to whether the other person is:

i   somebody you know very well

ii   a colleague you know quite well

iii   a complete stranger

Possible answers

Invitation

i   How about a film?/Fancy a film?

ii   Like to come to the cinema?

iii   Would you like to come to the cinema?

Request

i   Give us a hand with this case./Help me with this will you?

ii   Can you give me a hand with this case, Bill?

iii   Would you mind helping me with this case?

Enquiry

i   What's the time?/Time check, please.

ii   What's the time, Bill? / Have you got the time, Bill?

iii   Could you tell me the time?

Personality

a–c   Students work in pairs and then report to the group.

d   Students work in a group.

Possible answers

i   He seems to vary what he says according to who he is talking to, perhaps because he wants to be liked by everybody.

ii   I think she gives an appearance of sincerity in what she says but in fact is not trustworthy.

iii   He talks to you as if you're a small child, perhaps because he has difficulty relating to people normally.

iv   He spoke as if he was talking to another Englishman, rather than a foreigner. He's often insensitive to other people's needs or problems.

v   She kept giving people orders and correcting their mistakes – she's rather bossy by nature.

vi   She talks and acts spontaneously as if not worrying about what other people think of her. She's just herself.

vii   What he says gives an impression of friendliness, but I don't know what he really thinks or whether he really likes me.

viii   I didn't get a chance to speak. She isn't really interested in what other people have to say and is rather overbearing.

ix   He is using overfamiliar (sexist) language with a woman he has just met, particularly as she is a woman of some social importance.

Suggested supplementary question

To what extent is it absolutely normal and necessary to be 'all things to all men'? If you aren't, it creates a lot of problems, doesn't it?

4   POINTS OF VIEW IN POETRY

Students work in a group.

Suggested question

Do you think it is possible to have commercial, cultural or educational contacts and to give economic, medical or technological aid without somehow interfering?

5   ARGUMENT BY POSTCARD AND POSTER

Students work as a group. In (c) also consider what has been added to the poster by feminists, as well as the original message of the poster against the fur trade.

C   LISTENING ACTIVITIES

1   The *theme* is prejudice, attitudes and preconceived ideas. The *objective* is to help students become more aware of their own attitudes and to stimulate natural, adult discussion.

    The activity should be based on initial reaction, and tape should not be re-played in this case. Students are not asked to justify their answers but to think about why they have answered in such a way.

    The teacher is not involved in correction. If a student has not understood a word, other students should be encouraged to explain (in English).

2   The *theme* is points of view/standpoints. The *objective* is to provide practice in general and specific listening comprehension and to encourage development and fluency.

    The activity requires pre-study of questions, accurate listening, note-taking and discussion based on factual information. The teacher should be aware of signals from students who seem to be confused. However, the teacher, where possible, should allow discussion before prompts or correction. The tape can be played again if students seem to need another opportunity to listen.

Possible answers:

a   illness, allergies, hay fever

b   sneezing, red eyes, irritation, watering eyes

c   The 15-to-23-year-olds. They have more to lose, as they are sitting examinations or applying for jobs.

d   Examinations usually occur in the months when allergies such as hay fever are most common. Pupils and students who suffer from hay fever are disadvantaged during examinations.

e   He says that such remedies have side effects which interfere with normal life.

f   Mr Giles believes that natural remedies are harmless and do not interfere with normal life. However, they will help sufferers if they are taken in time.

Tapescript

1

a   politicians

b   Miss World

c   garlic

d   examinations

e   grandparents

f   video

g   chocolates

h   computers

i   dogs

j   teenagers

2

Anna Hastings	Good evening. This is Anna Hastings and it's time for 'You and Your Health'. We have a seasonal offering for you and an expert on allergies, Geoffrey Giles, to commiserate with sufferers. Geoffrey Giles.
Geoffrey Giles	(monumental sneeze followed by snuffle) My apologies. That wasn't a rehearsed performance. It's just that I can't stop sneezing at this time of year. My eyes go red and they water. People who don't know me wonder what I've been up to. When they ask, 'What's the matter with you, Geoff?' I normally sneeze again. (Voice indicating sore throat) Ah, well. It's worse for the young ones. Not the babies so much. They don't usually suffer before they've reached their first birthday. Unless they're destined for a life of allergies.
Anna Hastings	You mentioned 'the young ones', Mr Giles. What exactly do you mean by young?
Geoffrey Giles	Good question. 'Young' is one of those words that I find difficult to define . . . Fuzzy . . . woolly . . . Like fat or rich or disabled. . . .
Anna Hastings	What you're saying is that it depends on your point of view. And I agree. It's a good topic for another programme. But to get back to *our* topic . . . is there any evidence that certain age groups suffer more than others?

Geoffrey Giles	Thank you for reminding me. I tend to get carried away. Well, yes. There are certain age groups. For example, the fives to fifteens. It's unattractive and debilitating. The five-year-olds have runny noses, and the older children can't compete in field sports or tennis.
Anna Hastings	But they do get over it, don't they? I mean no one sneezes all year.
Geoffrey Giles	Some do, some don't. On the whole, it's very seasonal. But the sneezing season is also the examination season. The fifteen-to-twenty-three-year-old pupil or student suffers a real disadvantage. It's a fact that a 1985 survey showed that a majority of teachers advocated changing the traditional examination times to a season when the pollen count is not so high.
Anna Hastings	That's certainly one suggestion. But isn't there medication for hay fever sufferers? Surely there are tablets or injections . . .?
Geoffrey Giles	Of course, there are. Any sufferer can buy brand names over the chemist's counter. But what about side effects? Antihistamines are widely used, and the consumer often finds that he's drowsy, can't concentrate, is unusually thirsty. Driving or using dangerous equipment is usually warned against. These tablets can conflict with other medication.
Anna Hastings	You are painting a very gloomy picture.
Geoffrey Giles	Not at all. The answer is natural remedies. Homeopathic and biochemic. Life can continue normally and they will do you no harm. There is only one thing to remember. To be effective, treatment should be started about five to six weeks before you expect an attack.
Anna Hastings	That's a very strong statement, Mr Giles . . . Would you mind explaining why you are sneezing?
Geoffrey Giles	My own stupidity. I began the treatment too late.

D STRUCTURE AND LANGUAGE USAGE

1 THE LANGUAGE OF OPINION

Possible answers

a

i The Board's view is that the changes are indispensable. In the Board's view the changes are indispensable.

ii The Board is convinced that the changes are indispensable.

iii The Board sees the changes as indispensable.

b

i But nobody's asked (us) what our attitude to them is/about our attitude to them.

ii But nobody's asked (about) our opinion of them!/what our opinion is of them!

iii But nobody's consulted us!/But we haven't been consulted!

c

i In my opinion it's just another cost-cutting exercise!

ii As far as I'm concerned it's just . . .

iii I regard it as just another . . .

d

    i   We strongly protest at . . .

    ii   We (strongly) condemn the broadcasting . . .

    iii   We strongly object to the . . ./We object in the strongest terms to . . .

e

    i   . . . community to express its condemnation of this kind . . .

    ii   . . . community to denounce this . . .

    iii   express its revulsion against this . . .

f

    i   . . . all their time disparaging other people's efforts.

    ii   . . . time being scornful of other people's efforts.

    iii   . . . spend all their time knocking other people's . . .

g

    i   . . . victims earns our respect.

    ii   We applaud Bob Geldof's . . .

h

    i   . . . I have always disagreed with the . . .

    ii   . . . always disapproved of . . .

    iii   always been in disagreement with . . .

    iv   always been critical of . . .

i

    i   We wish in the strongest terms to register our disapproval of the use . . .

    ii   We wish to strongly condemn/wish strongly to condemn . . .

j

    i   I'm sorry but we object to being . . .

    ii   . . . we take exception to being . . .

    iii   We will not/cannot allow ourselves to be . . .

2   YOU MIGHT HAVE MENTIONED IT EARLIER!

Students work as a group.

Possible answers

a

    i   You might have phoned/let me know!

    ii   You should have rung/let me know!

    iii   You could have phoned to say you weren't coming!

b

    i   You needn't have said that/been so unkind.

    ii   You shouldn't have said that/been so unkind.

    iii   You could have been a bit kinder/kept quiet.

c

    i   You were supposed to have it ready by today/to have had it ready by today./It was supposed to be ready by today.

    ii   You should have had it ready by today./It should have been ready by today.

    iii   You were to have had it ready by today./It was to have been ready by today.

d
- i   She will always involve other people.
- ii I wish she wouldn't involve me/other people./I wish she hadn't asked me.
- iii She ought to mention it herself/talk to her boss about it herself/fight her own battles.

e
- i   What am I supposed to do?/How am I supposed to help?
- ii What can I do?/How can I help?
- iii I wish he hadn't asked me.

f
- i   Does he/she have to come (this weekend)?/Why did you have to invite him/her this weekend?
- ii He/she would want to come this weekend./You would invite her this weekend./It would be this weekend.
- iii Must you invite him/her this weekend?/Must he/she come?/He/she must have known I'd planned something else.

3 DISCUSSION

Students work as a group. Items a–f are often used to 'introduce' an opinion. Elicit varied suggestions from the group.

Possible answers (examples only)

a   . . . there is no alternative.

b   . . . he cannot continue without substantial financial support.

c   . . . it's just a waste of time.

d   . . . it's got a lot of advantages.

e   . . . he's got to be a lot more flexible.

f   . . . it's to my ultimate advantage.

7 IN THE NEGATIVE

Themes	Disasters and fiascos, success and failure, managing interactions, the negative sides of good qualities, the different ways of saying 'No'
Functions	Adducing causes, 'disarming', apologising, discussing human qualities, responding negatively to requests, expressing unwillingness
Structures	Negative forms, conditionals, future in the past, modals (past), passives (past), supposed to, I'd rather you (went). We wish you had (seen). Hardly, almost. It's better to . . .
Phonology	Syllable stress denoting form and usage.

Noun	Verb
☐	☐
reject	reject
☐	☐
discard	discard
☐	☐
contrast	contrast
☐	☐
discount	discount

Note that all of the above examples are formed with prefixes.

Lexis	reject (v), discard (v), exclude, repeal (v), back out, fail, suppress, cancel, quash, rescind, break off, turn down, give up, stop (v), deny, withdraw, sever, decline (v), discount (v), refuse (v)

A READING TEXTS

1 READING TEXT A

Clive Ponting was a civil servant for fifteen years until he resigned in 1985 after passing documents on a defence matter to a Labour MP.

DHSS: Department of Health and Social Security.

The lobby system: the system by which selected journalists are given briefings by Cabinet members on the understanding that they do not name the politicians concerned.

2 QUESTIONS ON THE TEXTS

Suggested supplementary questions

Supplementary to (a) and (b): What degree of secrecy is Clive Ponting in favour of, do you think?

d Encourage students to find vocabulary items that Clive Ponting employs with a negative implication here, rather than obviously pejorative words such as 'poor', 'deviousness', or 'bad'.

Possible answers

wall of secrecy; inward-looking; insiders; magic circle; public relations material; doctored; compliant; fed; slanted; tendentious; tunnel vision; warp.

Text B

Before 1971, £1 was divided into 20 shillings and 240 pence: 10/6 was therefore about 52 pence in the modern decimal currency, but of course it was worth considerably more in the period the story is set in.

b

Possible answers

sprawling inelegantly; contemptuously; afraid of; animal.

Both texts (extension)

Since both texts deal with the suppression of truth, teachers might wish to start a discussion as to which circumstances justify this, whether in international, national or personal affairs.

B COMMUNICATIVE ACTIVITIES

1 WHAT GOES WRONG?

Students work in pairs. Ensure that students have plenty of time to think about their answers. It is particularly important that students should make full use of the Study Notes.

> i   Titanic disaster, 1912.

Suggested supplementary questions

Would the *Titanic* tragedy be less likely in modern conditions? (radar, satellites, better rescue services)

Possible factors

Overconfidence on the part of the *Titanic*'s builders and captain. Inadequate lifeboat provision. The fact that warnings received by radio were probably not passed to the bridge. The fact that at that time ships' radios were not manned 24 hours a day. The absence of radar.

> ii   Opera House, Sydney, Australia.

Suggested supplementary question

How would the individuals concerned in this kind of fiasco get on together?

Possible factors

The difficulty of costing such a revolutionary design. Mistakes in the original architect's plans. Problems with contractors. 'Political' interference. Personality clashes?

> iii   Tenerife (1977, world's worst air disaster)

Suggested supplementary question

How would the individuals involved – air traffic controllers, pilots, and passengers respond to the situation before the accident?

Possible factors

Overworked air traffic controllers. The fog. The presence of extra aircraft at the airport because of the diversions. The impatience of the KLM pilot. (This was officially established as the cause. He started his take-off before getting permission.)

> iv   Chernobyl, 1986

Possible factors

Insufficient supervision to check that safety regulations were being observed. Inadequate training. In addition some Western scientists believe that design faults were also to blame.

> v   *Today* (launched 1986)

Possible factors

Bad market research. Inadequate financial backing. Not the right mix of information and entertainment. The fact that there are too many newspapers competing for a declining readership and a fixed amount of advertising.

2 WHAT MAKES FOR SUCCESS OR CAUSES FAILURE?

Students work in pairs.

a Give students ample time to think about their answers and, if possible, introduce other subjects that are closer to the students' interests or experience than those given in the exercise.

Possible answers

i	*Successful*	*Unsuccessful*
		Mumble or have a very monotonous delivery.
	. . .	Give rambling, shapeless lectures.
	Give an 'overview' and relate the lecture to the rest of the subject.	. . .
	Provide plenty of background information – handouts etc.	No handouts or background information.
ii	Sees himself or herself as a friend as much as a parent of a teenager.	. . .
	. . .	Doesn't take an interest in or participate in anything that he or she does.
	. . .	Treats the teenager as a child.
	. . .	Doesn't respect his or her individuality.
	. . .	Nags and criticises all the time.
iii	. . .	His/her characters are rather unreal.
	. . .	His/her plots are contrived and a bit 'shaky' sometimes.
	He/she writes convincing, realistic dialogue.	. . .
	Is able to hold the reader's interest from the first page to the last.	. . .

3 THE OTHER SIDE OF THE COIN

Treat the three parts of this exercise in an increasingly lighthearted way.

a Students work as a group.

Possible answers

    ii   careful; mean!
    iii   frivolous; never takes anything seriously; flippant
    iv   secretive; sly?
    v   talkative; superficial?
    vi   indecisive; passive
    vii   obstinate; wilful
    viii moody; vulnerable

b   Students work in pairs.

c   Students work in pairs.

4   WAYS OF SAYING 'NO'

Students work in pairs.

Possible answers (examples only)

a

    i   I don't think that will be possible.
    ii   I wish I was in a position to help you.
    iii   The answer's 'No'. I'm very sorry.

b

    i   Look, I wish we were in a position to say 'go ahead'.
    ii   Sorry, Jim, but it's out of the question./I think the answer's going to have to be 'No'.
    iii   Sorry, Jim, but no way. (colloquial)/No, sorry, Jim, but it's not on. (colloquial)

c

    i   Look, you're very sweet, Jim, but . . .
    ii   We wouldn't be happy together.
    iii   No, Jim, it's not a good idea.

d

    i   I'll see.
    ii   I'd rather not.
    iii   No, I can't, I'm sorry.

e

    i   We'd prefer you not to.
    ii   We'd much rather you didn't.
    iii   No, I must ask you not to go ahead with it.

5   MANAGING INTERACTIONS

a   Students work in pairs.

Possible answers (examples only)

    i   I hope you don't mind my asking, but how much did you pay for it?; Would you mind if I asked how much you paid for it?
    ii   Look, Jane, I know you're very busy, but do you think you could possibly get one more letter finished tonight?; Jane! Dear wonderful Jane – do you think you could possibly fit in one little letter before you go?

iii   Some of you will say you've seen it all before but . . .; Now, you might say this is nothing new, but . . .

iv   I'm not interrupting anything, am I? . . .; Hope I haven't interrupted anything . . .

v   Look, I realise it's a bit late to phone, but you see I need to know when the meeting starts tomorrow; Look, I do hope I haven't woken you up or anything, but the problem is I need to know what time tomorrow's meeting starts.

vi   I know it's none of my business, but shouldn't you check it with the Managing Director?; It's nothing to do with me, but wouldn't it be better to check it first with . . .?

vii   Now, you know I wouldn't interfere, but are you absolutely sure that acting is for you?; Of course it's your choice, but are you quite sure you're suited?; . . . sure it's right for you?

viii   I realize there will be some disagreement with this, but . . .; Not all of you will agree with this, but . . .; Some of you may well disagree with this, but . . .; Not everybody shares this view, but . . .

ix   You will be wondering, perhaps, when I will be getting to the subject of my talk . . .; You're probably wondering when I will get round to the subject . . .

x   As you know, I don't pretend to be an expert on . . ., but. . . .; Whilst not pretending to know a great deal about . . ., I would like to say that . . .

b   Students work as a group. (Obviously different cultures will have different ways of 'disarming'.) Treat the discussion and role-play as a 'fun' activity and if possible introduce other situations of greater relevance to the students involved.

Possible answers (examples only)

i   An intimate, friendly tone of voice, a smile and warm eye-contact.
ii   A smile, a shrug of the shoulders, a nod.

6   LANGUAGE GAMES

Students work as a group.

a

Treat this as a fun activity. Start the game off by yourself, firing fifteen questions at individual students in turn. You try to get him/her to say 'yes' or 'no'. If he/she manages not to use these words, it is a clear round and scores a point. The essence of the game is speed in order to cause mistakes, maintain interest and create enjoyment. At a suitable point hand over to a student quizmaster (preferably one of the more able). Encourage him/her to maintain a fast pace.

An alternative is to divide the group into two equal teams, with one member from one group quizzing one from the other in turn. A clear round scores one and the team with more clear rounds wins. Once again make sure fast pace is maintained.

b

Answer

What a wonderful bird the frog is
When he sits; he almost stands
When he leaps he almost flies
He has hardly got any sense
He's got hardly any tail either,
When he sits, he sits on what he almost hasn't got.

C LISTENING ACTIVITIES

The *theme* is managing interactions and the different ways of saying no or using negative behaviour. The *objective* is to help students discriminate between different kinds of verbal behaviour and to determine how appropriate they are.

The activity begins with the students' personal experience and moves on to an analysis of taped interactions. The teacher should monitor group work and write up relevant group comments. In activity 3, students are asked to listen, use the interaction chart from Unit 5 and discuss their reactions.

Possible answers

1

b   The child may be demonstrating his independence or demonstrating against authority. The patient may neglect to take tablets because she hasn't understood the importance or because she has other priorities. The secretary may be demonstrating resentment without being verbally assertive. The student may become submissive and feel that there is no point in discussing his work with the teacher.

2

Responses.

a   submissive

b   assertive

c   aggressive

d   manipulative

3

Dialogue a: The customer is aggressive.
Dialogue b: The traveller is submissive. The man is manipulative.
Dialogue c: Employee 2 is aggressive.
Dialogue d: Customer 1 is assertive.
                The waiter is aggressive.
                Customer 2 is submissive.
Dialogue e: The employee is submissive.

Tapescript

2

Responses

a   I'm a terrible failure, aren't I? I'll stay late to make up for it.

b   Yes, I know. I've explained that my child comes first and we have agreed on flexible hours.

c   You should talk. You're always late . . . unless the boss is in.

d   Oh, come on, Pete. I've covered for you in the past. It's your turn now.

Dialogue a In the shop

Customer	I've come in for a book you should have in stock. The title is *Interpersonal Skills in Nursing*. I can't wait for it.
Shopkeeper	It's a specialist-interest book, isn't it?
Customer	Well, I suppose you could say the uninformed would not be asking for it.
Shopkeeper	I'll need the name of the author and publisher.
Customer	Surely that's your responsibility. Are you in business or are you not?

Dialogue b

Traveller	Please, can you help me? I'm trying to find Platform 6.
Male 1	Come along with me. Are you on your way to Kent?
Traveller	I don't know. I'm just waiting to be met. You see, my son usually catches this train and we'd arranged to meet on platform 6 but my eyes aren't very good and . . .
Male 1	Well, if your son's coming that'll be all right then. Have a good journey.
Male 2	You got out of that one, didn't you?
Male 1	Yes, but I'm not proud of it. I really tried to get rid of her, didn't I? A bit of support and a lot of false reassurance.

Dialogue c

Employee 1	Hear you've got a new car . . . all the new dashboard bits plus. How about a lift home?
Employee 2	I've had just about enough of you, you pushy twit. Don't suppose you remember what happened last time I gave you a lift? Disappear before I push your nose in.

Dialogue d In the restaurant

Customer 1	Waiter, this isn't what I ordered. I'm afraid I don't eat meat. Vegetarian, you see.
Waiter	I haven't got time to discuss your way of life. Do you want it or don't you?
Customer 2	Thank you, we'll have it. George, we can leave the meat. Just push it to one side.
Customer 1	That isn't the point. When I pay for a meal I expect to be served what I've ordered . . . and with courtesy. Take this away, waiter, and bring me the risotto I ordered.

Dialogue e In the office

Boss	You'll be working late tonight, Jones. We have a deadline to meet and it's all hands to the wheel.
Underling	But . . . but, Mr Carruthers . . . It's awfully short notice and actually it's my wedding anniversary. My wife is expecting . . .
Boss	Easily solved. Give her a ring. That's that, then.
Underling	Whatever you say, Mr Carruthers.

D STRUCTURE AND LANGUAGE USAGE

Students work as a group.

1   DID IT HAPPEN OR NOT?

Do this as a round-the-class exercise.

Possible answers

a   No, they didn't go.

b   No, they didn't take them.

c   Yes, they did.

d   No.

e   Yes.

f   No. (the preference concerns a future event)

g   No.

h   No.

i   No.

j   No.

2   BUT HE DIDN'T . . .

Do this as a round-the-class exercise, encouraging students wherever possible to suggest more than one possible way of completing the sentence. (There are obviously possibilities other than those in the box.)

Possible answers

a   refused; turned it down; (wouldn't); (couldn't be persuaded)

b   he's given it up; he's given up smoking; he's stopped.

c   was turned down; was rejected; withdrew; (didn't get it); (wasn't successful); (was unsuccessful)

d   discard it; reject it; refuse to play with it; stop playing with it
    cancelled; cancelled it; withdrew; backed out; (pulled out)

f   withdrawn; rescinded; refused; cancelled

g   repealed it

h   was rejected; was turned down; was refused

i   was quashed; (was cut); (was reduced)

j   he denies it; (he says he had nothing to do with it)

k   they have been suppressed; they have not been allowed; permission has been withdrawn.

l   broken off; severed; cut

m   refused; rejected; turned down; withdrawn

n   backed out; cancelled

3   DIFFICULT NEGATIVES

Do this as a round-the-class exercise.

Grammar note

Note that in (g) 'This has not been the case for long' means 'The situation changed a short time ago' whereas 'This has not been the case for a long time' can mean 'The situation changed a long time ago.'

Possible answers

a   We don't think so either.

b   I don't think it's a very good idea: (I think it's a pretty bad idea.)

c   You'd better not go to the doctor's.

d   Don't anyone open the door!; No one open the door!

e   We don't expect to win easily.

f   They haven't got enough supplies (yet).

g   This has not been the case for long.

h   We haven't got far to go (now).

i   I'd rather not work in London if I have the choice.

j   This doesn't apply yet to some of the people working here.

k   I don't suppose anyone knows the answer; I suppose no one knows the answer.

l   I shouldn't think the car's ready yet; The car won't be ready yet.

Preparation of Texts A and B should be set as homework before the next Unit is attempted.

8 EMPHASIS

Themes	Ideological emphasis, first impressions, interviews, selecting information for emphasis
Functions	Expressing and eliciting opinions. Giving personal information. Expressing emphases. Discussing priorities. Responding enthusiastically to offers, invitations, suggestions and enquiries. Reassuring
Structures	'What' in exclamatory sentences. Intensifiers, emphasisers and maximisers. It's . . . that really matters. What really matters is . . . . The point I'm trying to make is . . . Inversion. □ □
Phonology	Spelling and pronunciation. *ph* [f] as in phonology, emphasis, □ □ □ □ □ physics. *acc* [ak's] as in accentuate, accent, access, accelerate, □ □ □ □ accident. However, *acc* [ak] as in accord, account, accommodation. □ □ *us* [ʊːʒ] as in unusually, illusion.
	Stress and intonation. Unstressed 'what' and 'that' as in 'What really *matters* is . . .' 'It's . . . that *really matters*.' Falling intonation in emphatic responses as in 'Yes, I do !' 'Yes, indeed !' Intonation of invitations, suggestions, enquiries, as in 'Like a coffee?' 'Have some □ more sweet?' 'You like horror films, don't you?'
Lexis	emphasis, put a lot of emphasis on, emphasise, stress (v and n) lay / put stress on, accentuate, point up, give prominence to, prominent, put the accent on, crucial, give the impression that, very, indeed, amazingly, definitely, really, simply, absolutely, surprisingly, extremely, unusually, certainly, unbelievably, terribly, so, incredibly, only, totally

A READING

1 READING

Text B vocabulary

A 'hooligan' is a commonly used word for a (young) troublemaker; a 'rowdy' is similar in meaning but emphasises the noisy aspect of their behaviour; 'aggro' is a colloquial term for aggression, especially in social encounters and relationships. 'Hard-case' and 'nutter' are explained in the text and have a more limited currency.

2 QUESTIONS ON THE TEXTS

Text A

Possible answers

a   It has an / anti-materialist / anti-capitalist / socialist / Marxist / emphasis.

Suggested supplementary question

What are the particular emphases that give clues to the broad ideological emphasis?

Text B

a   Peter Marsh tries to emphasise the 'social order' of the football terraces, whereas to an outsider they might seem to represent the breakdown of social order.

Teachers may like to ask their students to re-read Text A of Unit 3 (Logical relations) because the contrast between that text and Text B of the present unit would be most productive of further discussion.

Suggested supplementary question

Clearly Peter Marsh has more direct experience of football crowds than the *Daily Telegraph* leader-writer – shouldn't we therefore take notice of his more positive voice?

B COMMUNICATIVE ACTIVITIES

1 TALKING ABOUT IMPRESSIONS

a   i   Students work as a group.

Possible answers

Eyes, hands, how relaxed they are, how much eye-contact they give, how close they stand, how loudly or quietly they talk, how much they smile, whether they are gentle or aggressive.

ii   Students work in pairs.

Possible answers

By phone	By letter, memo etc.	Other people's conversation	Seen on TV
Relaxed voice? Educated? warm	Kind of language	Respect or disrespect, admiration or dislike	Dress, personality

iii   Students work as a group.

Possible answers

At important meetings, at interviews, at important family events.

Suggested question

Do you try to impress people wholly in their terms?

iv   Students work as a group. They think about their answers individually and then compare them with what the rest of the group consider to be the most striking features of each student's appearance, body language, behaviour etc., taking care to restrict these to what would be noticed at a *first* meeting.

v   Students work as a group.

Possible answers

Yes, we are/overinfluenced by physical factors/too responsive to physical appearance; we should pay more attention to character and mind.

b   Interviews

1   Students work as a group.

Possible answers

i   knows her/his subject; answers/readily/with hesitation/willingly/rather reluctantly/fluently/confidently.
    Is he thrown (confused) by some of the questions?

ii   has/a smart appearance/an outgoing personality; able to/defend his point of view/argue cogently/persuasively; she/inspires confidence/is able to 'field' questions well/is good at getting on with people; is good with people; interacts well.

iii He/she has got a negative/positive attitude towards them; he/she regards them as 'enemies'.

iv He or she is reluctant/perfectly willing to enlarge on subjects/points.

2 Students work as a group.

Suggested supplementary question

What do you try to emphasise about your personality and character?

3 Students work in pairs.

Possible answers

i The interviewee can't answer the questions put to him/her. He/she waffles. (colloquial) (waffle: to talk very vaguely and at length) He/she seems tongue-tied.

ii The applicant is badly dressed; he/she seems uncooperative/aggressive/'difficult'.

iii The applicant seems to/resent questioning/dislike the interviewers.

iv The interviewee/appears unwilling to enlarge on anything/gives the briefest possible answers/answers in monosyllables.

2   IT MUST BE EMPHASISED THAT ....

Students work in pairs – give them plenty of time to prepare their answers to this activity either in pairs in class or individually as homework. Then do it in two parts:

a Elicit the main points for emphasis (italicised below in the possible answers) with the help of the suggested questions.

b Discuss with the group the actual language that might be used.

i

Suggested supplementary questions

a/b

i What would the public need to be reassured about regarding the President's health? What might the Press Officer say about the President's condition and behaviour soon after the operation?

Possible answers

No cause for concern: The President's doctors stress that/the President is in excellent general heath/the President is amazingly fit for a man of his age.

Minor operation: The President's doctors emphasised that there are thousands of such operations every day.

Total success: pronounced a 100% success by doctors.

Faster than average recovery: 'joking with nurses only hours after the operation'; 'amazing powers of recovery' say doctors

Already back in control: bedside consultation with advisers working on his papers on the phone to his Secretary of State for a lengthy consultation.

ii

Suggested questions

What fears would the workforce have in this kind of situation? How could the new parent company reassure them? In what further ways could the company demonstrate that it deserved the workers' support?

Possible answers

There are *absolutely no plans to close the plant or reduce the workforce*. This factory has an *important part to play* in the company's worldwide operations.
New plans: There are indeed plans to expand production at this site.
Business as usual: In the meantime the company would continue to operate exactly as before, with the very minimum of changes.

iii

Suggested supplementary questions

What situations would be most damaging to the company? What does the company need to say has already been done?

Possible answers

The contamination was limited to one small batch of cartons. All of this suspect batch has now been located and destroyed under the supervision of government-appointed Health Inspectors. *Mothers can therefore continue using our products with complete confidence* – as they have been doing for the last 58 years.

iv

Suggested supplementary questions

What aspects of the cash-flow problem would the company wish to stress? Which other points could they underline that might put the cash-flow problem in a better light?

Possible answers

The overall position is good despite the recent downturn. Sales are 17% up on last year.
The cash-flow problem is very temporary, and the company enjoys an extremely amicable relationship with its financial advisers.
The outlook is bright, and a big deal with a high street retail chain is about to be clinched.

v

Suggested questions

Imagine you are the girl in this situation. Which points would you feel it necessary to emphasize?

Possible answers

There's nothing to worry about . . . nothing's happened . . . really, Mum. . . . Stayed with a girl she met . . . Coming back tomorrow morning . . .

3   PROVERBS, SAYINGS AND QUOTATIONS

Students work in pairs.

a   Assign proverbs to pairs according to the number of pairs in the group.

Possible answers

i What really matters is money. It's money that really matters. If you've got a lot of money you can get things done. Money gives you power.

ii Having knowledge isn't enough: the important thing is knowing an influential person who can help you. What really matters is the people you know. You might think knowledge is the important thing but in fact it's the people you know.

iii What's important is knowing how to live a simple life. It's not money but knowing how to live simply that matters.

iv The important thing in a wife is what she says rather than how she looks. What's important in a wife is her conversation, not her physical appearance.

v It's too late to do anything now (once the milk is spilt), so it's no use being unhappy about it. You can't do anything about it, so you might as well stop worrying.

vi It's better to accept less now than to try to get more and lose everything. Take what you can get rather than risk everything trying for more.

vii (We can't be sure. Here are two possible interpretations.) What's important is the present. Don't spend your life looking forward to the future; live life now, today!

viii What's important in life is manners. The single most important part of education is (the inculcation of) manners.

Possible supplementary question

What do you think manners are?

ix Don't count on things turning out exactly as planned.

x You can only judge things by results./What's important is results rather than intentions./It's results that matter.

4   HAVE THEY GOT THEIR PRIORITIES RIGHT?

This activity could be treated fairly quickly and lightly. The group might also like to find and discuss *local* examples of selective advertising.

Notes on vocabulary

i SW1 (pronounced 's''w' one) stands for South-West One and is an important area of central London. 'Privately educated' and (vii) 'boarding school education' refer to the public-school system, which is independent of the state educational system and supported mainly by fees. Approximately one in fifteen British schoolchildren are educated in this way. (Note that in the USA a public school is the same as a state school in the UK.)

iv NW3 is a fashionable residential area of north-west London.

C LISTENING ACTIVITIES

The *theme* is the expression of personal emphasis through use of syllable and sentence stress for contrast and definition of meaning. The *objective* is to encourage discrimination of attitude based on stress and intonation, together with general and specific comprehension.

The activity should be conducted by allowing freedom of conjecture. Students should be encouraged to use the language of conjecture in pair and group work. For example, must be, can't be, could be, should be . . .

The teacher should wait until students have had an opportunity to provide answers before offering help. Remember that this is a comprehension exercise. Fluency of speech is not required; neither is absolute grammatical correctness.

1
Suggested answers

a   This is a family discussion between father, mother and son.

b   The subject is the son's future career. He has just received excellent 'A' level results.

c   The father seems to want his son to achieve prestige and social status. The mother appears to be conventional and unwilling to realise that her son is now able to make his own decisions.

d   Possible paraphrases:
    i   You talk too much, Helen. What I want to say is more important.
    ii   I'm going to tell you what you should do.
    iii   I disagree. I refuse to accept your values and judgements.
    iv   At last I can be independent.
    v   I understand only too well. You have kept me from doing what I've wanted to do all my life.

2
Suggested answers

a   i   Polite questions (concealed commands); for example: 'Perhaps you'd like to sit over there.' 'Would you care to begin?'
    ii   Abrupt and exploratory questions. Open but inappropriate. 'Just how much do you know about the history of nursing?' 'What can you tell us about . . .?'
    iii   Open, process questions requiring the student to give his own opinion and allowing time. 'I wonder whether anyone has suggested . . .?' 'Could you tell us a little more?'

b   Henry responded to the attitude of the questioner. When he thought he was required to produce facts, he did so. When he was encouraged to express his own ideas, he did so.

c   Speaker 1: to establish her authority.
Speaker 2: to mould Henry into her model of a student.
Speaker 3: to find out what Henry wanted to do.

3

a   This will be an open discussion. Students may relate the comments to their own past experiences and should be allowed to express their feelings. There are clues in the tape. For example: 'You appear to be exceedingly nervous.' 'Please try to answer questions directly.' 'I wonder whether anyone has suggested that a career in nursing might be a waste of your academic ability.' 'My concern is to recruit students and keep them.'

b   Finally, students are asked to do a role-play. They will be using their own emphases to decide whether or not Henry should be accepted. Replay the tape if there has been a time gap. Part 1 is significant to Henry's attitude and decision.

Tapescript

Part 1

Mum	Well done, Henry. And you *deserve* it. All that hard work. *No* football, *no* discos, no *fun* . . . why, you even . . .
Dad	*Do* be quiet, Helen. Now let me think. Three 'A' levels. Two A's and a B. You could be a *doct*or. Fancy that, Helen. The boy could be a *doct*or.
Henry	I don't *want* to be a doctor. I'm going to be a *nurse*.
Mum	Now you just listen to me, Henry Groves. *Real* men don't become *nurses*. Why can't you use some sense?
Dad	*Sense? I'll* give you sense. Sense is being a famous consultant . . . heart transplants and that . . . seeing your name in headlines. *That's* sense.
Henry	Not for *me*, it isn't. I don't have to study medicine just because *you're* ambitious. Now I can make up my *own mind*.
Mum	I can't understand what makes you go on like this. You *must* see our point of view.
Henry	I *do*. I most *certainly* do. But I'm still going for my interview tomorrow.

Part 2

Angela Maude	Come in. (pause) Oh, *do* come in. Mr *Graves*, isn't it? Perhaps you'd like to sit down down over *there*.
Henry	Mmm. Thank you. My name is *Groves*, actually. *Henry* Groves.
Angela Maude	Now make yourself comfortable, Mr, er, uh, *Groves*. I'll introduce you to the other members of the panel. On my left is Miss Pritchard, who is an expert in helping our students get through exams with flying colours. On my right, Mr Morgan. He is concerned with student welfare and counselling. I, as you probably know, am the Senior Tutor, Angela Maude. Now that you're settled, we'd like to ask you a few questions. Miss Pritchard, would you care to begin?
Miss Pritchard	Of course. Welcome to our School of Nursing, Mr Groves. Now, just how much do you know about the history of nursing?
Henry	(long pause) Sorry. I don't really know how to answer that question.
Miss Pritchard	Let me rephrase it. What can you tell us about Florence Nightingale?
Henry	(parrot style) Florence Nightingale was the founder of nursing as we know it today. Until Miss Nightingale introduced a code of conduct, nursing was haphazard and held in low esteem. This code was best exemplified during the Crimean War, when Miss Nightingale managed to reduce cross-infection and also to save the lives of many amputees.

Miss Pritchard	Well memorised, Mr Groves. In your own words, how does this history relate to nursing today?
Henry	I just want to be a nurse . . . as soon as I can qualify. I want to do something for humanity, ease suffering, comfort the dying.
Miss Pritchard	You appear to be *exceedingly* nervous. Please try to answer questions directly.
Angela Maude	Perhaps Mr Morgan would like a few words.
Mr Morgan	Delighted. May I call you Henry? You have a distinguished school record, Henry. Three very good 'A' levels. I wonder whether anyone has suggested that a career in nursing might be a waste of your academic ability.
Henry	Lots of people.
Mr Morgan	Could you tell us a little more?
Henry	For a start, there was the headmaster. 'The country needs scientists,' he said. 'Nuclear physicists, electronic engineers, computer programmers. *Any*one can do nursing.'
Mr Morgan	And how did you feel then?
Henry	First, I felt sorry for him. And then I was angry. It's *my* life, isn't it? I want to be a nurse, not a criminal. From the way people talk you'd think . . .
Mr Morgan	Yes, Henry. I could almost finish your sentence. I've travelled the same road. I'd like to ask you a question from my own experience. How do you think you could survive as a male in a fundamentally female society?
Henry	Don't worry about *me*. I've burnt all my bridges.
Mr Morgan	Thank you for being so honest.
Angela Maude	We shan't keep you much longer, Mr . . . Henry. There are a few practical details to discuss, however. I see from your notes that you've been living at home. Bearing in mind that student accommodation is limited, would you be prepared to continue that arrangement?
Henry	Definitely *not*.
Angela Maude	*I* see. Well, thank you for coming. We'll be in touch within the next few days. Have a safe journey.

Part 3

Angela Maude	(gasp) That was without a doubt the most amazing interview I've ever held. What did you think of him, Flora?
Miss Pritchard	Hmmph. Has an amazingly good memory. Don't think much of his appearance. Surprisingly little to say for himself, considering the passion for nursing. Not sure he knows his own mind.
Angela Maude	Right, Flora. We'll go into your impressions shortly. You might like to listen to what Dai has to say. *I* certainly would.
Mr Morgan	I've been thinking about that young man. He was surprisingly diffident when he talked to you, Flora.
Miss Pritchard	What are you suggesting? Do you by any chance mean that I was intimidating?
Mr Morgan	Not at all. Simply thinking aloud. There's more to Henry than meets the eye. I must be careful about any recommendations. I identify with him . . . Reminds me of myself at his age.
Angela Maude	What exactly do you mean, Dai? 'There's more to Henry than meets the eye?'

Mr Morgan	Just that young Henry has a hidden agenda. He hasn't told us everything . . . something he seems to be holding back. Nevertheless, I like him. I'd like to see him given an opportunity.
Angela Maude	That's all very well, Dai. But my concern is to recruit students and keep them. We all know how disastrous the drop-out rate is. Plays havoc with staffing *and* the budget. In my opinion we should only consider definite projected passes.
Miss Pritchard	If you want to know my opinion, Henry will be a prickly and awkward student. Possibly a trouble-maker. He's frighteningly keen. *Not* a pass.
Angela Maude	So what is your collective opinion? We have 16 applicants for 12 places. Should we offer Henry a place?

D STRUCTURE AND LANGUAGE USAGE

Students work as a group. Treat this as a round-the-class exercise.

1 THE LANGUAGE OF EMPHASIS

Possible answers

a

   i   The professor emphasised that he didn't want to attend the seminar.

   ii   The professor stressed that he didn't want to attend the seminar.

b

   i   My school put a lot of stress on team sports and self-reliance.

   ii   A lot of emphasis was put on team sports and self-reliance at my school.

c

   i   The importance of the family is stressed in Islam.

   ii   The family is crucially important in Islam.

   iii   The family is of crucial importance in Islam.

d

   i   His inexperience in this field was accentuated by the presence. . .

   ii   The presence of so many experts at the meeting pointed up his inexperience in this field.

   iii   What made his inexperience in this field more obvious was the presence of

        . . .

e

   i   The new campaign will put the accent on fitness and health./The accent will be on fitness and health in the new campaign.

   ii   Great stress will be put on/laid on fitness and health in the new campaign.

f

    i   The totally empty background gives prominence to the lively activity in the foreground.

    ii   The totally empty background makes the lively activity in the foreground more prominent.

    iii   The totally empty background gives emphasis to the lively activity in the foreground.

2   TREAT THIS IN THE SAME WAY AS THE PREVIOUS EXERCISE

Possible answers

a   Very friendly people, the Pearsons.
Really friendly people . . .
What friendly people the Pearsons are!
The Pearsons are so friendly.
The Pearsons are amazingly friendly.

b   Very nice place, Brighton.
Extremely/really nice place, Brighton.
What a nice place Brighton is!
Brighton is such a nice place!
Brighton is so nice!

c   Very interesting book, *The Name of the Rose*.
What an interesting book *The Name of the Rose* is.
Unusually/extremely/really interesting book, *The Name of the Rose*.
The Name of the Rose is an incredibly interesting book.

d   Very good point you've made.
That's an excellent point you've made.
What an excellent point you've made.
That's a very good point indeed!

e   Never again must the sequence of famine, starvation and death happen.
The sequence of famine, starvation and death will not be allowed to happen again.

f   Not for one/a moment do I doubt what you say.
I certainly don't doubt what you say for a moment.
I don't in any way doubt what you say.

g   Only by investing in jobs will we beat unemployment.
It is only by investing in jobs that we will beat unemployment.
Investing in jobs is the only way to beat unemployment.

3   BUT OF COURSE . . .

Allow students to think about what they are going to say, then elicit increasingly enthusiastic responses like this:
Student 1   Do you like Indian cooking?
Student 2   Yes, I do.
Student 3   Yes indeed!
Student 4   I absolutely love it!

Possible answers:

a   Yes, please!
     I certainly would!
     I'd really love one!

b   Thanks I'd like to!
     I'd really like to, thanks!
     What a good/nice/great idea! Thanks!

c   Yes,I do!
     Of course/indeed I do!
     How could I forget you?

d   Yes, I did.
     Yes, very much indeed!
     Loved every (single) moment!

e   Yes, I do!
     Very much, yes!
     Never miss one!

f   Thank you, I will.
     Yes, please, it's very nice.
     I'd love some more, it's marvellous.

g   Yes, do!
     Of course you can!
     Of course, we'd love you to!

h   Yes, let's!
     Yes, I'd like to!
     What a great idea, I'd love to!

i   Yes, please!
     Thanks, I could do with one!
     I'd love one, thanks!

j   Yes, please!
     Thank you, I would!
     That's very kind of you. Thanks!

4   USING MORE COLOURFUL LANGUAGE

Give students plenty of time to consider their responses.

Possible answers

a   They were (absolutely)/furious/beside themselves with rage/livid!

b   It was (absolutely) fascinating!

c   He's/crazy about her/in love with her/infatuated with her.

d   She's/amazingly beautiful/stunning!/stunningly beautiful.

e   I'm absolutely/finished/shattered/exhausted.

f   It was/absolutely dreadful/incredibly awful/unbelievably bad.

g   It/was(so)delicious!/quite marvellous!

h   We had to wait/for ages/hours/hours and hours/hours on end.

i   It was hilarious/We couldn't stop laughing!

E WRITING ACTIVITIES

a
   i   Only by going there yourself will you find out what it's really like.
   ii   It's only by going there yourself that you will find out what it's really like.

b
   i   Only in an absolute emergency should you ring that number.
   ii   Only in an absolute emergency should that number be rung.

c
   i   Under no circumstances should those controls be touched.
   ii   Those controls should not be touched under any circumstances.

d

      What you forgot to mention was that this would be your last visit here.

e
   i   Only very recently have they begun to appreciate the possible consequences.
   ii   It is only very recently that they have begun to appreciate the possible consequences.

f

   i   It was only after weeks of negotiation that we eventually came to an agreement.
   ii   Only after weeks of negotiation did we come to an agreement.

g

      Not one member of the platoon survived.

h

      What I'm trying to say is that I think it's feasible.

i

      The point he's making is that these arrangements can't be sorted out overnight.

2   EXTENSION: TEXT IMPROVEMENT

Suggested answer (example only)

The great majority of people have a dread of interviews: the experience of having every detail of your personality, knowledge and career under the closest scrutiny is an utterly unnerving one. They feel totally vulnerable and know they are taking part in a lottery the result of which will crucially influence the whole of the rest of their lives. Just one careless word or facial expression might make all the difference between success and failure and what is particularly depressing to the unsuccessful candidate is to know that even though everybody freely admits that an interview is often merely a matter of luck, they will nevertheless take the result completely seriously and apportion blame or admiration accordingly. What is intensely painful to learn, after an unsuccessful interview as you limp away from the scene of the battle promising yourself that never again will you submit to such indignities, is that the winner was a compromise candidate or that it was all an inside job from the very beginning.

Additional suggestions for written work

If there is a need for extra written reinforcement of work done in this unit the following may be attempted:

B2 It must be emphasised that (page 128)
Write out what three of the speakers would actually say in (i)–(v).
(page 128).
Write out the emphatic version of 2a–d.

Preparation of Texts A and B should be set before the next unit is attempted.

9 IN THE MIND

<table>
<tr><td>**Themes**</td><td>Academic disciplines, attitudes and qualities of mind, dreams, connotations, misunderstandings</td></tr>
<tr><td>**Functions**</td><td>Expressing and eliciting opinions, expressing responses to poetry, making invitations and requests, pre-invitations, relating dreams and daydreams, discussing connotations, contrasting fields of study</td></tr>
<tr><td>**Structures**</td><td>Past continuous, as if . . . Verb patterns: deduce, conclude, posit, imply, assume, realise, imagine, start, get to (colloquial), keep</td></tr>
<tr><td>**Phonology**</td><td>In words of Greek origin, English pronunciation may be very difficult, even for native Greek speakers.

Some useful hints are: In words beginning with *sc*, for example, sciences, scene, scintillate, the *c* is silent. This also applies to some other mid-word clusters such as discipline.

☐   ☐

<u>Ph</u> is pronounced [f], as in physics, physician.

☐   ☐   ☐

<u>Psy</u> is pronounced [saɪ], as in psychology, psychic, psychiatry. Note also *ch*, as in chemistry [kemɪstrɪ] or chaos [keɪɔs]

☐   ☐   ☐   ☐   ☐ ☐   ☐</td></tr>
<tr><td>**Lexis**</td><td>deduce, deducible, correlate, correlation, infer, inference, postulate,

☐

conclusion, get the idea, bear in mind, have in mind, have an idea (about . . . bring in mind, change one's mind, be uppermost in one's mind, call to mind, cross one's mind, slip one's mind, suggest</td></tr>
</table>

A READING TEXTS

1   READING

Text A is shorter than Text B but is considerably more difficult. Ensure that students have ample time for preparation.

Text A

Coleridge, Samuel Taylor (1772–1834)   British poet, critic, and philosopher.
Linnaeus, Carolus (Carl von Linné) (1707–78) Swedish botanist.
Darwin, Charles (1809–82) British naturalist, author of *The Origin of Species*, 1859.
Halley's Comet   A comet which appears every 76 years. Discovered by Edmund Halley (1656–1742), who was the first to realise that comets had periodic orbits.

B COMMUNICATIVE ACTIVITIES

1 ACADEMIC DISCIPLINES

a   Students work in pairs.

Possible answers (examples only)

Subject	Studies	Seeks to explain	Benefit to society
Psychology (human)	The workings of the human mind; the study of individuals interacting with their social and physical environment	Human thought, feelings and behaviour	Provides data for e.g. psychiatry, education, criminology
Economics	The production of goods and services, their distribution, exchange and consumption	Movements in prices, exchange rates, production costs, demand for labour, raw materials, etc.	Helps the government to manage the country. Provides data for business studies, sociology, etc.
Anthropology	The biological, social and cultural origins and development of humankind	How human civilisation has developed	Helps our understanding of men and women in groups. Provides data for linguistics, social psychology, environmental studies.
Linguistics	Language in all its forms	How language develops and changes. How languages 'work'. How human beings acquire language etc.	Helps our understanding of speech defects, language learning, bilingualism
Physics	The motion and interaction of matter and the transformation of energy	'The mechanics of the universe.' The nature of the interrelationship between matter and energy	Provides input for civil and mechanical engineering, defence industries, manufacturing industry, electronics etc.

b   Students work as a group.

Suggested supplementary questions

Why isn't it a 'scientific' subject? What divides a 'truly scientific' subject from the others? What are the criteria?

c   Students work in groups. In order to do this and questions (d) and (e) well, students must have adequate time to prepare their answers. There is no need for students to limit themselves to the subjects in (a).

Possible answers (examples only)

These are names of branches of disciplines mentioned in (a):

Psychology: social psychology, applied psychology, industrial psychology, experimental psychology
Economics: econometrics, applied economics, micro-economics, macro-economics
Anthropology: cultural/social anthropology (*cultural* anthropology principally in the USA; *social* anthropology in the UK), physical anthropology
Physics: nuclear physics, solid-state physics, astrophysics

d   Students work in groups.

Suggested supplementary questions

Have there been any fashionable theories or schools of thought in (economics) in recent years? Could you tell in what way they broke with the past?

e

Possible answers (examples only)

an analytical mind; a mathematical bent; patient observation; perspicuity of mind; a capacity for abstract thought

2   ATTITUDES AND QUALITIES OF MIND

Students work as a group.

a
   i   The Rupert Brooke poem could be said to be chauvinist or jingoistic in its extremely romantic and almost embarrassing patriotism.
   ii   'Bleeding' is a mild swearword; 'went west' is colloquial here for 'died'.

Suggested supplementary questions

Does Sassoon mean what he says in the last line? What's it called when we sneeringly say the opposite of what we think, for example 'You're very kind' when we really think they're being unkind, unhelpful etc.? (Answer: Sarcasm.)

b

Possible answers (examples only)

   i   philosophical; reflective; detachment
   ii   indifference to risk
   iii   strictness; self-denial; 'dryness'
   iv   single-mindedness; devotion
   v   rationality; incredulity; tendency to doubt
   vi   otherworldliness; a striving for the ideal
   vii   detachment; spiritual enlightenment

c   The purpose of this activity is to give rise to discussion on the subjects mentioned rather than to elicit clear-cut answers.

Suggested supplementary questions

Aren't libraries, beautiful architecture and paintings culture? But buildings aren't religion? What about the people who say they've seen ghosts? Would love still exist if human beings had no minds?

3   DREAMS

Students work as a group.

a   Give students time to prepare their thoughts on this topic either as homework or, failing that, during a few minutes of 'thinking time' during the lesson. If possible begin with an example of any kind of dream from your own experience. Students should ideally be in a *relaxed mood* when they do this activity.

Suggested supplementary questions

Do you think dreams mean anything or are they just the result of the mind ticking over (like a car engine)? If you dreamt that someone was going to be killed in a car crash, would you warn them to drive carefully that day, or would you not bother?

b   *Daydreams*

Once again it would be advisable to introduce the subject with an example from your own experience.

Suggested supplementary question

Do you daydream more if you're worried, or under stress of some kind, or more if you're relaxed?

4   CONNOTATIONS

Students work as a group. Encourage students' imagination here and, wherever possible, try to elicit more than one suggestion for each item.

C LISTENING ACTIVITIES

The *theme* is awareness of barriers to listening and communication and develops Unit 6, (Standpoint). The *objective* is to further develop students' awareness of meaning and appropriacy.

The activity requires interpretation of stress, intonation, and the shared meaning of words.

The teacher has an important introductory role. In 1, should students have difficulties, the teacher must use the appropriate intonation to suggest the functions stated. This should lead on to 2 and allow students to discuss their own interpretations.

3

Possible answers

The answers to dialogues 1–5 are open, but the teacher should check that students have listened to the example. Make sure that answers are written in figures. Elicit random answers by a brainstorming session. The point is to demonstrate differences.

4

a

Tapescript

Suggested stimuli

i	*Why* weren't you *listening*? (Defensive)
ii	What were *you* doing during the lecture?
iii	What did you think about the *lecturer*?
iv	Why weren't you paying *attention*?
v	Where *were* you when I rang last night? Why didn't you answer the phone?

Tapescript Example

Man	Before you begin this activity, it's only fair to give you an example and let you have a go. Listen to two women speculating about their new neighbours.
Woman 1	By the way, Helen . . . have you met the new people at number 46? They say he has a super job.
Woman 2	No, but I've seen their cars. How much do you think he earns per year?
Man	He has a super job. How much does a man in a super job earn per year? Write your answer in figures. £15,000? £50,000?

Dialogue 1

Man 1	Have you seen the new unit manager? Bit of a dolly bird, wouldn't you say?
Man 2	Very smart. Very slick. Smells expensive, too. How much would you say she takes home after tax?

Dialogue 2

Child 1	My mum's really old. How old is yours?
Child 2	Ancient. But she says she's middle-aged. What do you think that means?

Dialogue 3

Woman	Just listen to Ella with that disgusting cough. Sounds like a chronic bronchitic.
Man	Well, they do say she's a heavy smoker. How many fags do you suppose she gets through from breakfast to bedtime?

Dialogue 4

Man 1	George is looking a bit teased out, don't you think?
Man 2	Not surprising, is it? With that large family.
Man 1	People keep talking about his large family. What is a large family, anyway?

Dialogue 5

Woman	Charles, what shall I do about this anniversary party we're having in a fortnight? How many people have you invited?
Man	(fudging) Oh, quite a few.
Woman	I don't really know what you mean by 'quite a few'. How many people do you think should be asked to a silver anniversary party?

i   I *was* listening.
ii   I was daydreaming.
iii He was talking down to us.
iv   What makes you think I wasn't paying attention?
v   I must have been having a shower.

D STRUCTURE AND LANGUAGE USAGE

Students work as a group.

1   Do this as a round-the-class exercise.

Possible answers

a
i   Robert didn't actually know the last word, but he was able to deduce it from the rest of the crossword/he deduced it from the rest . . .
ii   Robert didn't actually know the last word of the crossword, but it was deducible from the rest . . .

b
i   The incidence of some hormonal problems and participation in long-distance races have been correlated; The incidence of some hormonal problems has been correlated with participation in long-distance races.
ii   A correlation has been established between the incidence of some hormonal problems and participation in long-distance races; It has been discovered that there is a correlation between the incidence of some . . .
iii A link/correlation/connection has been posited between the incidence of some hormonal problems and participation . . .

c
    i   NASA scientists working on ice-covered lakes in Antarctica have deduced that sufficient heat . . .
    ii   NASA scientists working on ice-covered lakes in Antarctica have come to the conclusion that . . .
    iii   NASA scientists working on ice-covered lakes in Antarctica have postulated/postulate that sufficient . . .

d
    i   The tax authorities made the inference that a tax avoidance scheme was being operated when . . .
    ii   The tax authorities concluded that a tax-avoidance scheme was being operated when . . .

e
    i   A recently published survey of 700 localities in London suggests that material deprivation and ill-health are (closely) correlated; A recently published survey of 700 localities in London correlates/correlated/has correlated material deprivation with ill-health.
    ii   A recently published survey of 700 localities in London suggests there is a causal connection between material deprivation and ill-health; A recently published survey of 700 localities in London establishes/posits/a causal connection between. . . .

f
    i   (Reading between the lines of the advertisement), Jane inferred they were looking for someone younger.
    ii   (Reading between the lines of the advertisement) Jane decided/thought/concluded that it implied (that) they were looking for someone younger; Jane decided (that) the advertisement implied (that) they were looking for someone younger.

2   Students work in groups. Do this as a round-the-class exercise.

Possible answers

a   Sorry it completely slipped my mind.
b   What exactly do you have in mind?
c   I don't think he has any idea about this kind of work.
d   Her sculptures call/bring Giacometti to mind.
e   Bear in mind that he's very new to the job.
f   I'm sorry, it just didn't cross my mind that you'd want to come.
g   They've somehow got the idea that you're there to help them.
h   I've changed my mind about (buying) these books. Would you mind taking them back?
i   Financial matters were obviously uppermost in their mind.

3   WHAT'S ON THEIR MINDS?

a   Students work as a group. Encourage students to offer several possibilities for each exchange and to use the ellipted forms studied in Unit 4.

Possible answers (examples only)

i   (I) wondered if I could borrow £10; Could you lend me £10?; It's just that/the thing is I haven't had time to get to the bank; Could you spare me £10?

ii   Just wondered whether you would like to come round?; There's an Ayckbourn play on in town, like to come?; Thought you might like to do something together?

iii   (No) I don't think/so/we will.
OK if I borrow/have/take it?

iv   It's OK, why?/Never been there./Not bad . . .
There's a two-day seminar and someone ought to be there; We'd like you to attend a two-day seminar; Like to go to a marketing seminar/an exhibition?

b   Students work in pairs. Get the pairs first to prepare and then to act out their three-part exchanges.

Possible answers (examples only)

i   Do you like the music of Vivaldi?
Yes, I do.
Only there's a concert at the Festival Hall next Thursday. Would you like to come along?

ii   Ever been to Jeddah, Peter?
No, I haven't.
Well, now's your chance. We need someone to go out next month.

iii   How busy are you on Friday week, Barbara?
I'm not absolutely sure, why?
Jane and I would like to have you round to dinner.

iv   Got anything on on Thursday night, Paul?
Er . . . no.
We've got an urgent job if you could do with some overtime.

10 NOT QUITE CLEAR

Themes	Controversies, ambiguities, wordplay, misunderstandings and jargon
Functions	Expressing opinions, asking for clarification, requesting elaboration, expressing doubt, expressing possibility, talking about confusions and misunderstandings
Structures	Verb patterns: assume, forget, expect, remember, realise. Past perfect. Future continuous. May, might, might well, could, should, need ☐
Phonology	Stress shift for meaning in compound words. For example: ☐landing ☐light (a light which is used for landing a plane); ☐landing ☐light (a light which is on the landing of the stairs); ☐smoking-☐compartment; smoking ☐compartment; smoking-room (a room where smoking is allowed); smoking ☐room (a room which is on fire and smoking); ☐swimming-coach (a coach who teaches swimming); swimming ☐coach (a coach who is swimming, but who may teach any subject).
Lexis	possible, possibly, possibility, arguably, presumably, conceivable, mix-up, mix up, distort, distortion, fudge (v), obscure (v), confuse, confusion, chance (n), impression, misapprehension, mistaken (in), take (= assume), foresee

A READING TEXTS

1 READING

Text A has five main points; remind students of the need to exercise their enumerating skills when they recount the main points of the text.

When reading Text B, students should be particularly encouraged to apply what is described there to their own experience of meetings and indeed communications of all kinds.

B COMMUNICATIVE ACTIVITIES

1 MORE DETAILS

Students work as a group.

a   Encourage use of the future continuous in (i), (ii) and (iii).

Possible answers (examples only)

i   Who would I have to see? Where would I stay? Why isn't the General Manager going? Why doesn't the GM want to go this time? What's the itinerary? What will my brief be? Is anyone else going? Will anyone else be going?

ii   Where will you be staying? How are you/they travelling? How many teachers will be going with you/them? How much will it cost?

iii   Could you give me a more precise idea of what the job entails? Who would I report to? Approximately how many people would report to me? Could you give me an idea of promotion prospects within the company? What sort of salary will you be offering? Is a company car provided? Is there a company pension scheme?

iv   What do they do exactly? What kind of work do they do? Are they connected with any religious group or are they independent?

v   What sort of experience has she got? What was her last job? Where has she worked? Can she use a word processor? How old is she?

vi   What will this reorganisation involve? How will it affect us? Will there be any redundancies? Are there plans to close down any of our operations?

b   *Not the whole story*

Students work in pairs. Encourage the free expression of opinions here and also perhaps humorous suggestions for some of the items.

Possible answers (examples only)

i   What the beach is really like; How noisy the hotel is; How far away the beach is; How thin the walls are; That the hotel is still being built.

ii   They don't mention the cost (in higher taxation?) of their proposals; They don't say exactly how their policies will be implemented; They understate the problems they will encounter with their policies.

iii   The bad points of the person that has died; the bad sides of his or her character; how badly he or she treated other people; the havoc he or she caused in other people's lives.

iv   What your boss/future colleagues are really like; Why exactly your predecessor left.

v   Dampness; what the neighbours are like; the disadvantages of the location.

2   WHERE DO WE DRAW THE LINE?

Students work as a group. Explain the meaning of 'to draw the line' and encourage a lively discussion. Focus attention on the second part of the instructions: 'stating any doubts you have . . .' and try to elicit sentences such as 'The problem is that some children need more discipline than others' or 'There are children who respond well to "freedom", but it's difficult to decide beforehand how he or she will react . . .!'

Introduce local controversies when they are more appropriate and omit any from consideration that you judge would not be suitable or productive.

Suggested supplementary questions

a   Which is it more dangerous to overdo, discipline or freedom?

b   Would you say you worked to live or lived to work? Is one or other of these attitudes to work on the increase, do you think?

c   What about subjects that could be taught more practically, such as learning a foreign language, but which are still treated in a very academic way at some universities?

d   How do you feel about some married women choosing to follow a career rather than become a mother?

e   Are you forgetting that these people contribute to their benefits through taxation and insurance?

f   Are you savouring every moment or patiently waiting? Are the two sides of the argument mutually exclusive?

5   'INTER-COMMUNICATING METHODOLOGISTS'

Students work as a group. The purpose of this exercise is to make students aware of the obfuscating effect of jargon.

This 'advertisement' appeared in *The Guardian* on 1st April 1986 – April Fools' Day. It makes fun of the kind of job advertisement often made by politically left local authorities such as the Greater London Council (abolished in 1986) whose job descriptions seemed extremely vague and which carried out policies of positive discrimination (= discriminated *in favour*) with regard to ethnic minorities, the disabled etc.

Try to maintain a serious approach to this 'joke' advertisement for as long as possible, keeping the students mystified by the obscurity of the jargon and eliciting from them as many requests for clarification as possible.

Vocabulary note
A WASP is originally an American term meaning a White Anglo-Saxon Protestant.

a   Most of these items of vocabulary are examples of widely used (sociological) jargon that some sections of society object to as imprecise and the result of confused thinking.

1   (Before students know the advertisement is a joke:)What kind of applicant would the job suit? If you were doing this job would you know what you ought to be doing?

2   (Afterwards:) What is the author of the advertisement making fun of (a) in terms of jobs? (b) in contemporary language?

6   MORE THAN ONE MEANING

Students work as a group.

Suggested answers

a

i   The teenage son is married to his mother.
     The woman is married and has a teenage son.

ii   Cleaners who dry-clean in one hour.
      Sixty very small cleaners.

iii   The extension to the M23 has no foundation.
       Reports that cracks have appeared in the extension are untrue.

iv   Jane is the woman on Richard's left.
      Jane is the woman on Richard's right (but from *our* point of view on his left).

v   This food is too hot to eat.
     I don't feel like eating in weather like this.

vi   Gym shoes are the only acceptable footwear.
      Everybody must be naked except for gym shoes.

vii   See what you're like on TV.
       Attack TV.

viii   I had a boyfriend once, but someone stole him from me.
        I had a boyfriend once, but someone cooked him in boiling water.

ix   Married soldiers were kissing their wives goodbye and unmarried soldiers were kissing their girlfriends.
      Married soldiers were kissing their wives and girlfriends goodbye.

x   I had left the light on outside my bedroom.
     I had left the airport landing-lights on.

c
Example answers only

i   Wife, and mother of a teenage son; wife with a teenage son.

ii   One-hour cleaners. (Of course the meaning would be clear if it was *spoken*.)

iii   . . . a County Council spokesman said the report was completely without foundation; . . . a County Council spokesman said it was not based on fact.

iv   Jane is the woman on the left of Richard as we look at them.

v   I don't like eating in this heat.

vi   Gym shoes are the only acceptable footwear.

vii   This is an example of *intentional* ambiguity and so it is inappropriate to try to remove the ambiguity.

viii   : . . but someone stole/pinched (colloquial)/took him from me.

ix   . . . soldiers kissing their wives or their girlfriends goodbye.

x   As (vii).

7 INTENTIONAL AMBIGUITY IN ADVERTISEMENTS

Students work as a group. Advertisement (b) is, of course, wordplay rather than ambiguity in that it exploits the fact that 'wait' and 'weight' are homophones. Advertisement (c) is only very superficially ambiguous in that the two sentences would be read and written very differently: 'See the economy 'breakdown on page 5712.' and: 'See the economy' break down on page 5712.'

Suggestion for further work

Ask students to collect further examples from magazines, newspapers, record sleeves etc. and analyse the kind of ambiguity or wordplay in class.

C LISTENING ACTIVITIES

The *theme* is the difficulty we all have in arriving at a common interpretation and the dangers of ambiguity. The *objective* is to help students realise how often assumptions are made, particularly in listening, and to relate the exercise to students' own experience.

The activity requires listening twice, with thinking time allowed between the two. Students are allowed to change their answers after the second listening. Working as a group, they should then try to agree on and justify their answers.

The teacher should facilitate rather than dominate group work and discussion, and finally, provide answers.

1

Answers

a   False. The ship was chartered by a scientist but not necessarily a biologist.

b   False. We don't know that this is true. Was the scientist born in the North Country or merely working there?

c   False. We don't know this to be a fact, although it is hinted at.

d   False. It is not stated that the white bird was, in fact, an albatross.

e   True.

f   False. We only know that the crew protested *and* that they quoted an old superstition.

g   False. He gave permission to *kill* the bird, but not necessarily to shoot it.

h   False. The mishaps occurred after the killing, not as a result of it.

i   True.

j   It is not stated that the net caught on the bottom of the boat.

k   False. We don't know that the captain fell as a result of the storm.

l   False. We don't know that Jackie Larson's rib was the one broken. Furthermore, the statement says 'his rib'. How do we know that Jackie was a man?

m   False. He became seasick for the first time.

n   False. We have no way of knowing whether the ship actually landed.

o   False. It was not stated why the cook left his job.

2

Encourage students to exemplify, from their own experience, and to suggest ways that assumptions may be clarified.

Tapescript

A distinguished North Country university scientist chartered a ship and sailed eastward. One day during the voyage a large white bird was sighted and the scientist asked permission to kill it. He claimed that the white albatross is often found off the coast of New Guinea. He wanted the bird as a specimen for his university museum. The crew protested against the killing of the bird and reminded the scientist of the old sea superstition linking the killing of the albatross with bad luck. Nevertheless the captain granted permission to kill the bird and the bird was killed.

These mishaps happened after the event: The engines failed three times. The net caught on the bottom and was ripped. A storm arose and the captain fell overboard. A rib was broken when scientific aide Jackie Larson fell down a hatch ladder. The scientist became seasick for the first time in his life. Lost gear forced the ship to head for land. The cook left his job.

D STRUCTURE AND LANGUAGE USAGE

Students work as a group.

1

    Do this as a round-the-class exercise.

Possible answers

a

   i   The share boom may be bottoming out; It may be that the share boom is bottoming out.

  ii   There's a possibility that the share boom is bottoming out; It's a possibility that . . .

 iii   The share boom might well be bottoming out.

b

   i   French involvement in the Middle East might have triggered these attacks.

  ii   French involvement in the Middle East has arguably triggered these attacks; Arguably, French involvement . . .

 iii   French involvement in the Middle East could possibly have triggered these attacks.

c

   i   Student grants may eventually be replaced by student loans; Student loans may eventually replace student grants.

  ii   Student grants might/may/could possibly be replaced by student loans; Student loans might/may/could possibly replace student grants.

 iii   It's (quite) conceivable that student grants will eventually be replaced by . . .; It's (quite) conceivable that student loans will . . .

d

    i   She could have been turned down because of her outspokenness regarding company policy.

    ii   She might have been turned down because . . .

    iii   Presumably she was turned down because . . .; She was presumably turned down because . . .

e

    i   There's a chance that some university philosophy departments will have to be closed.

    ii   It's on the cards that some university philosophy departments will have to be closed.

    iii   The stage may be reached when/where some university philosophy departments have to be closed.

2   **a**   The Treasury says the monthly figures have been *distorted* by the three days of national holiday; The Treasury says there has been some *distortion* of the monthly figures caused by the three days of national holiday; The Treasury says the three days of national holiday have caused/brought about/given rise to (some) *distortion* in the monthly figures.

    b   Of course it was an interesting talk, but I felt it *confused/mixed up* description and explanation; Of course it was an interesting talk, but I felt there was a *confusion* between description and explanation.

    c   The ministers have had serious disagreements, but there will no doubt be a *fudge* suggesting peace and harmony at the end.

    d   I think what happened was that there was a *mix-up* with some of the addresses; I think what happened was that the addresses of some of the letters were/got *mixed up*.

    e   All this empty verbiage *obscured* the real problem from people.

    f   I think there was some *confusion* about/as to/regarding what the purpose of the meeting was; Many people were *confused* as to what the . . .

3   Misunderstandings

Possible answers (examples only)

a

    i   They didn't realise the President was going to feed his cat.

    ii   They were under the impression that this was polite behaviour.

    iii   They thought they were doing the right thing.

b

    i   Mr Richards assumed he'd lit the gas.

    ii   He didn't realise he'd forgotten to light the gas.

    iii   He didn't remember that he hadn't lit the gas; He didn't realise he hadn't remembered to light the gas.

c

    i   The Saudis expected anything called wine gums to contain alcohol.

    ii   The Saudis were mistaken in thinking wine gums contain(ed) alcohol.

    iii   The Saudis were under the misapprehension that wine gums contain(ed) alcohol.

d

    i   The Finance Director's secretary assumed her boss would play his answerphone back; The Finance Director assumed the working breakfast was still on.

    ii   The Finance Director didn't think the working breakfast had been cancelled; His secretary thought her boss would play his answerphone back.

    iii   The Finance Director's secretary didn't foresee that her boss might not play his answerphone back.

e

    i   Debbie had no idea she was being dated.

    ii   Debbie was under the impression they were going as singles.

    iii   Debbie took it that she was being invited because Paul wanted a lift home.

4 WHAT DO YOU MEAN EXACTLY?

Possible contexts

c   Two people who have just seen a new play.

d   A committee discussing an imminent series of interviews.

f   A young couple.

g   Primary school teacher talking to parent about a little boy.

i   Spokesman on an industrial dispute.

When possible requests for clarification have been discussed, do this as a simulation exercise, with pairs taking the parts of A and B.

Possible answers (examples only)

a   Could you define 'natural language'? What is natural language?

b   In what sense exactly?; In which sense are you using the word?

c   In what way exactly?; In what sense?; How do you mean?

d   What do you mean by that?; Meaning?

e   In what way exactly?; How?; How does it do that?

f   What do you mean 'not so sure'?; How do you mean?; What does that mean?

g   How do you mean?; How does he do that?; How?

h   Why's that, then?; In what way?

i   In what way/sense?; Could you elaborate (on that)?